LAWS AND LEGISLATION

TRIBAL LAW AND ORDER

A PLAN TO ENHANCE TRIBAL JUSTICE

LAWS AND LEGISLATION

Additional books in this series can be found on Nova's website under the Series tab.

Additional e-books in this series can be found on Nova's website under the e-book tab.

LAWS AND LEGISLATION

TRIBAL LAW AND ORDER

A PLAN TO ENHANCE TRIBAL JUSTICE

JUDY CONLON
EDITOR

NOVINKA
New York

For permission to use material from this book please contact us:
Telephone 631-231-7269; Fax 631-231-8175
Web Site: http://www.novapublishers.com

Library of Congress Cataloging-in-Publication Data

ISBN: 978-1-63117-152-9

Published by Nova Science Publishers, Inc. † New York

CONTENTS

PREFACE

This book discusses the Tribal Law and Order Act's long term plan to build and enhance tribal justice systems as well as the Department of Justice's ability to clarify eligibility for certain grant funds.

Chapter 1 – In recent decades, Tribal Nations have faced significant problems in addressing public safety issues. Violent crime rates in Indian country are more than 2.5 times the national rate; some reservations face more than 20 times the national rate of violence. Some tribes lack the funding and infrastructure to address these problems. Indian country correctional facilities are inadequate in number and funding may not be sufficient for operations, maintenance and programming. In some Tribal Nations, there are insufficient alternatives to incarceration. In 2010 Congress passed the Tribal Law and Order Act (TLOA) to address these problems. The goal of TLOA is to improve public safety and justice systems in Indian country.

TLOA mandates that the Departments of Justice (DOJ) and the Interior (DOI) develop, in consultation with Tribal Leaders and tribal justice professionals, a long term plan to address incarceration and the alternatives to it in Indian country. DOJ and DOI obtained substantial input from tribal justice officials, including law enforcement, courts, and corrections. DOJ and DOI conducted a series of consultations with Tribal Leaders across the country; conducted focus groups with tribal justice officials; hosted webinars; created a multi-agency Work Group on Corrections ("Work Group") to provide recommendations on action steps; and drafted a Tribal Justice Plan (Plan) for public comment. Those comments were incorporated into the final Plan submitted to Congress.

Chapter 2 – Report of the United States Government Accountability Office on Tribal Law and Order Act: None of the Surveyed Tribes Reported

Exercising the New Sentencing Authority, and the Department of Justice Could Clarify Tribal Eligibility for Certain Grant Funds.

In: Tribal Law and Order
Editor: Judy Conlon
ISBN: 978-1-63117-152-9

Chapter 1

TRIBAL LAW AND ORDER ACT: LONG TERM PLAN TO BUILD AND ENHANCE TRIBAL JUSTICE SYSTEMS*

Department of Justice and U.S. Department of the Interior, Workgroup on Corrections

EXECUTIVE SUMMARY

TLOA Background and Overview

In recent decades, Tribal Nations have faced significant problems in addressing public safety issues. Violent crime rates in Indian country are more than 2.5 times the national rate; some reservations face more than 20 times the national rate of violence.[1] Some tribes lack the funding and infrastructure to address these problems. Indian country correctional facilities are inadequate in number and funding may not be sufficient for operations, maintenance and programming. In some Tribal Nations, there are insufficient alternatives to incarceration. In 2010 Congress passed the Tribal Law and Order Act (TLOA) to address these problems. The goal of TLOA is to improve public safety and justice systems in Indian country.

* This is an edited, reformatted and augmented version of a Department of Justice and U.S. Department of the Interior publication entitled Tribal Law and Order Act: Long Term Plan to Build and Enhance Tribal Justice Systems published August 2011.

TLOA mandates that the Departments of Justice (DOJ) and the Interior (DOI) develop, in consultation with Tribal Leaders and tribal justice professionals, a long term plan to address incarceration and the alternatives to it in Indian country. DOJ and DOI obtained substantial input from tribal justice officials, including law enforcement, courts, and corrections. DOJ and DOI conducted a series of consultations with Tribal Leaders across the country;[2] conducted focus groups with tribal justice officials; hosted webinars; created a multi-agency Work Group on Corrections ("Work Group") to provide recommendations on action steps; and drafted a Tribal Justice Plan (Plan) for public comment. Those comments were incorporated into the final Plan submitted to Congress.

Central Themes of the Tribal Justice Plan

The following major themes emerged from consultation and public comment:

- Establishing alternatives to incarceration should be the major focus.
- The Tribal Justice Plan should be implemented in consultation and collaboration with Tribal Leaders and should be flexible enough to allow tribes to develop strategies tailored to their specific public safety needs and tribal history and culture.
- The Tribal Justice Plan should coordinate federal, tribal, state and local government resources to support operations, programming in tribal justice systems, and critical infrastructure issues with tribal correctional facilities, fully mindful of the sovereign status of tribes in these coordination efforts.
- There should be greater coordination between DOJ and DOI with respect to awards for grants that may be used to construct tribal correctional facilities and multi-purpose justice centers (which may be provided by DOJ) and P.L. 93-638 contracts and self-governance compacts for funding operations (provided only by DOI). The Departments are committed to addressing the issue of coordination to address this and other issues related to detention in Indian country.

Tribal Leaders', Practitioners' and Experts' Recommendations for Key Considerations Underlying the Tribal Justice Plan

- ***Develop a system of alternatives to incarceration.*** Identify the points in the system where incarceration occurs, examine the reasons why, and explore alternative evidence- based practices to safely monitor the offender in the community.
- ***Make alternative interventions culturally specific to individual Nations.***
- ***Include after school and summer programs for tribal youth as part of crime prevention strategy***.
- ***Ensure that tribal jails comply with standards*** on such issues such as inmate classification, health services, sanitation, preventative maintenance, discipline, grievance procedures, offender services and activities, staffing and others.
- ***Include juvenile detention and treatment.*** Inventory existing funding and technical assistance resources for tribal youth across federal agencies; and develop training for community coalitions to support tribal juvenile detention facilities.
- ***Support regional partnerships with state and local entities to contract for bed space to improve capacity and sustainability.***
- ***Develop data-driven, comprehensive programming.*** Use planning data and validated risk assessment tools to assess key trends in tribal jail population and define critical programming and partners. Support research to identify effective methods in Tribal Nations.
- ***Apply jail standards to facility funding, construction and maintenance.***
- ***Develop and implement evidence-based reentry programs that include risk assessment tools and individual case management plans.***
- ***Locate more federal halfway houses on tribal lands to keep members connected to community and family.***

Action Steps and Recommendations

Six Month Goals

- DOJ will use resources from the Tribal Courts Assistance Programs (TCAP), Indian Alcohol and Substance Abuse Assistance (IASAP),

Drug Courts Programs, and Tribal Youth Program to support alternatives to incarceration programming.

- Share information with tribal courts about electronic alcohol monitoring bracelets (BIA).
- Offer funding and training and technical assistance for detention, alternatives to detention, and multi-purpose justice facility planning, renovation, and construction (DOJ).
- Explore potential resources to promote comprehensive programming (the Work Group).
- DOJ will support reentry activities through the Second Chance Act's Demonstration, Mentoring, Correctional Technology Jobs, Co-Occurring Substance Abuse, Family Treatment and Mental Health Disorders grant programs, and the Tribal Juvenile Detention and Reentry Green Demonstration Program.
- Explore strategies to facilitate and streamline tribal justice hiring, basic competency training, and securing clearance processes (DOI and Workgroup).
- Add other critical federal partners to support implementation of the Tribal Justice Plan, including agencies representing law enforcement, civil rights, victims, youth issues, family violence and defense (the Work Group).
- Continue to coordinate across federal agencies after the Tribal Justice Plan is completed and submitted to Congress.

Twelve Month Goals

- Explore the feasibility of creating a work release program for tribal members returning from federal incarceration and the potential impact of such a program on crime victims.
- Fund Tribal Probation Academies and explore assistance such as training for probation supervisors and training on planning and managing a tribal probation agency (DOJ).
- Expand the Juvenile Detention Alternatives Initiative (JDAI) to Indian country (DOJ/OJJDP).
- Enhance coordination of current federal funding for tribal corrections facility and multi purpose justice center planning, construction, transition, maintenance, operations, and programming.
- Coordinate funding of new construction to maximize success of these projects (DOI and DOJ).
- Create a peer advocate training program (DOJ/OJJDP, BIA, and IHS).

- Explore potential resources to assist high risk offenders or those needing specialized services (BOP, BIA and Federal Probation).
- Explore resources of BIE to address offender educational requirements.
- Coordinate federal reentry services in Indian country with the U.S. Probation and Pretrial Services Indian Country Steering Committee and with other federal, tribal and state agencies. Develop a collaborative strategy to enhance accessibility of federal funding and resources in the areas of alternatives, detention, and reentry for Tribal Nations.
- Create an online consolidated database on funding opportunities, resources, training and technical assistance (Work Group).
- Provide cross-agency training to emphasize the importance of multidisciplinary strategies to achieve best results from the Tribal Justice Plan.

The Work Group also made recommendations for enhancements in funding and creation of new resources in particular areas.

Conclusion

Tribal Nations face significant public safety challenges. TLOA provides a critical opportunity to acquire the tools needed to build effective alternatives to incarceration and to improve incarceration and reentry strategies. These strategies should be tribally led and based upon data and planning, with the help of federal agencies with the resources to support these goals. The Work Group is committed to implementing these Action Steps and Recommendations, and helping tribal justice systems to improve public safety.

Acknowledgments

The Tribal Law and Order Act (TLOA) has created a tremendous opportunity for Tribal Nations across the United States to enhance their tribal justice systems and improve safety in Indian country. Tribal vision and leadership set the priorities and informed the implementation of this Long Term Plan to Build and Enhance Tribal Justice Systems (Tribal Justice Plan). We are very grateful to all of the Tribal Leaders who provided input at the eight consultations on TLOA and the written comments. We are especially appreciative of the tribal justice officials who attended the three focus groups - their knowledge, expertise and commitment to safety in their Nations brought great insights. These Tribal Leaders and tribal justice officials will be critical partners in implementing the Tribal Justice Plan.

We also thank the federal agencies and staff that were a part of the Work Group on Corrections, who coordinated the outreach to Tribal Nations, provided content on webinars, meetings and the report and who identified ideas, resources and issues that informed the Tribal Justice Plan. They will continue to be critical partners in the implementation of the Tribal Justice Plan.

Finally, we want to acknowledge the support and leadership of other organizations who supported the development of the Tribal Justice Plan. Special thanks goes to the National Congress of American Indians and the National Criminal Justice Association for their support through the webinars, outreach and comments in developing the Tribal Justice Plan. We also thank EKMP, Crime and Justice Institute, American Indian Development Associates, Lamar and Associates, CSR Incorporated, and Education Development Center for their input and expertise in developing this Tribal Justice Plan.

SECTION 1: BACKGROUND

TLOA: History and Overview

Tribal Nations have historically faced significant challenges in addressing public safety issues. Recognition of this problem led to the passage of the Tribal Law and Order Act (TLOA) of 2010, signed into law by President Obama on July 29, 2010. TLOA seeks to address many of the challenges faced in tribal justice systems, to establish greater accountability for federal agencies responsible for prosecuting crime on reservations, and to provide tribes with tools to combat extremely high rates of crime. In signing the bill, President Obama remarked that it is "unconscionable that crime rates in Indian country are more than twice the national average and up to 20 times the national average on some reservations."[3]

A foundational principle in the development of tribal justice systems, and therefore in any consideration of changing those systems, is tribal sovereignty. Indian tribes exercise sovereign powers over their members and their territory. In legislation, case law and Executive Orders, the federal government has affirmed the political sovereignty of tribes and interacts with Tribal Leadership on a government-to-government basis. In current practice, including development of this Tribal Justice Plan, the government-to-government relationship is embodied by consultation and coordination between Tribal Leadership and federal agencies on issues that impact tribes.

Criminal jurisdiction in Indian country depends on a number of factors, including where the crime took place, the status of the alleged offender and victim (Indian or non-Indian), and the type of offense. The complexity of jurisdictional issues is a result of the Major Crimes Act, 18 U.S.C. § 1153, Public Law 83-280 as amended (P.L. 280), other federal statutes, and numerous federal court decisions. The Major Crimes Act provides for federal court jurisdiction for certain offenses committed by Indians in Indian country.[4] Pursuant to P.L. 280, the United States has transferred criminal jurisdiction over some reservations to states and authorized other states to assume either full or partial jurisdiction over crimes committed by or against Indians in Indian country.[5] Tribal sovereignty and jurisdictional authority are at the forefront of the recommendations in this Tribal Justice Plan.

TLOA: Legislative Charge for the Long Term Plan to Build and Enhance Tribal Justice Systems

Three sections of TLOA direct the creation of the Long Term Plan to Build and Enhance Tribal Justice Systems. Each of these sections directs that a plan must be submitted to Congress one year following the date of enactment.

TLOA requires the Secretary of the Interior (section 211(b)(5))[6] and the Attorney General (section 244(d)) to collaboratively develop the plan. In addition, it requires DOI and DOJ to consult with Tribal Leaders and tribal justice officials in the development of the plan. Specifically, the law states that the Departments of Justice (DOJ) and Interior (DOI) shall submit to Congress a long term plan to address incarceration in Indian country that addresses:

(1) a description of proposed activities for the construction, operation, and maintenance of juvenile and adult detention facilities (including regional facilities) in Indian country;
(2) a description of proposed activities for contracting with state and local detention centers, upon approval of affected tribal governments;
(3) a description of proposed activities for alternatives to incarceration, developed in cooperation with tribal court systems;

(4) an assessment and consideration of the construction of federal detention facilities in Indian country; and
(5) any other alternatives as the Secretary of the Interior and the Attorney General, in consultation with Indian[7] tribes, determines to be necessary.

Further, Section 241(g)(1) provides that the Secretary of the Interior and the Attorney General, in consultation with Tribal Leaders and tribal justice officials, shall develop a long term plan for the construction, renovation, and operation of tribal juvenile detention and treatment centers and alternatives to detention for juvenile offenders. This Section requires the Bureau of Indian Education (BIE) and the Indian Health Service (IHS) to coordinate with tribal and Bureau of Indian Affairs (BIA) juvenile detention centers to provide services to those centers.

Consultation and Outreach Strategy with Tribal Nations

The sections of TLOA that direct the creation of the Tribal Justice Plan require that DOJ and DOI consult with Tribal Leaders and seek the input of tribal justice officials, including tribal law enforcement, courts, and corrections. DOJ and DOI developed and implemented a multifaceted consultation plan to facilitate broad input from Tribal Leaders. In addition, DOJ and DOI sought broad input from tribal law enforcement, court and corrections officials.

- ***Consultations with Tribal Leaders***. DOJ and DOI, in partnership with other federal agencies, hosted a series of consultations with Tribal Leaders between October 2010 and May 2011. The seven consultations held between October and December 2010 related to TLOA overall,[8] while on May 10-11, 2011, DOJ and DOI co-hosted another consultation specific to the Tribal Justice Plan[9].
- ***Webinar education and dialogue sessions***. DOJ and DOI collaborated with the National Congress of American Indians (NCAI) and the National Criminal Justice Association (NCJA) on a series of webinars about the TLOA Tribal Justice Plan. These webinars provided a 30-minute presentation by subject matter experts, followed by a 60-minute dialogue period in which input was sought from Tribal Leaders and members. Topics included an Overview; Alternatives to

Detention; Detention Planning, Construction, and Operations; and Reentry. The webinars were recorded and posted on NCAI's TLOA resource page at tloa.ncai.org/webinars.cfm.

- ***Focus groups with tribal justice officials***. DOJ, DOI and federal partners hosted three focus groups with Tribal Leaders and tribal justice officials—including those from law enforcement, courts, corrections, social services, and treatment—to seek more in-depth input on the challenges facing tribal justice systems, promising strategies, gaps, resources, and the best ways to address needs. These events highlighted the expertise of practitioners who face these challenges every day and are developing innovative solutions.[10]
- ***Written comments solicited***. Tribal members and the public have been encouraged to send input about the Tribal Justice Plan to a special e-mail box, TellTLOA@usdoj.gov. The e-mail address has been advertised through the webinars, consultations, and focus groups. A draft Tribal Justice Plan was released from July 15 through July 21, 2011 for public comment. Over 40 comments were received, which were incorporated into the final draft of the Tribal Justice Plan.

Feedback from Tribal Nations

The outreach efforts generated important feedback that informed the Tribal Justice Plan and the strategies and recommendations included in this Plan. Tribal justice officials provided information about challenges that reflected their extensive experience and a rich set of strategies to overcome barriers. The following major themes emerged:

- ***Alternatives to incarceration are of primary importance***. Alternatives to incarceration (which could include treatment) should be the paramount objective in any plan to address the corrections aspect of public safety in tribal nations. Detention of tribal members should be a rare exception in the corrections context, where many of the offenders are suffering the effects of poverty, isolation and substance abuse.
- ***Tribal Leaders and federal agencies should work together***. The Tribal Justice Plan should be developed and implemented in collaboration with Tribal Leaders and not driven exclusively by

federal agencies. DOJ and DOI were encouraged to continue this dialogue through consultations and focus groups or similar meetings.

- ***A plan should be flexible enough to meet varying tribal needs.*** Tribal Leaders and justice system officials reiterated that recommendations and strategies should allow each tribe to address its safety and corrections needs according to its tribal history and cultural values. This is especially the case with tribal justice systems in Alaska (and other very remote locations) where the physical remoteness and extreme weather create additional complexities in operating tribal justice systems.
- ***Federal funding streams for alternatives, incarceration and reentry are limited and complex.*** Tribal Leaders and tribal justice officials reiterated the federal government's trust responsibility in operating tribal justice systems. They also noted that the current bifurcation of funding between the federal agencies makes planning and implementing strategies complex and noted that there are not enough resources to sustain the strategies of all federally recognized tribes.

Structure of Work Group on Corrections

TLOA requires that the Tribal Justice Plan be developed jointly by DOJ and DOI. Moreover, development of the Tribal Justice Plan required the joint involvement of the IHS, located in HHS, and DOI's BIE. To oversee the creation of the Plan, DOJ and DOI created a TLOA Work Group on Corrections (Work Group), which includes the following agencies:

- Office of Justice Programs, DOJ
- Office of Tribal Justice, DOJ
- Bureau of Prisons, DOJ
- Office of Civil Rights, DOJ
- Community Relations Service, DOJ
- Executive Office for U.S. Attorneys, DOJ
- National Institute of Corrections, DOJ
- Office of the Assistant Secretary - Indian Affairs, DOI
- Bureau of Indian Affairs, DOI
- Bureau of Indian Education, DOI
- Indian Health Service, HHS
- Substance Abuse and Mental Health Services Administration, HHS

- Department of Agriculture
- Federal Probation Service

The Work Group will continue to meet and coordinate implementation activities, and DOJ and DOI will seek to add new partners, consistent with the recommendations in this Tribal Justice Plan. Due to the impact of some of these recommendations, the implementation will also be coordinated with other workgroups and committees as appropriate.

Overview of the Tribal Justice Plan

The next three Section s of this Plan include:

- ***Section 2: Alternatives to Incarceration in Indian Country***. TLOA requires that the Tribal Justice Plan include an examination of activities in Indian country that facilitate alternatives to incarceration. Generally, alternatives to incarceration are programs, services, or supervision that allow an individual to avoid incarceration and remain in the community with effective mechanisms in place to ensure public safety.
- ***Section 3: Detention in Indian Country***. Tribal Leaders feel strongly that incarceration should be a last resort, but acknowledge that detention is appropriate for those offenders at high risk for recidivism[11] and violence. This Section explores Indian country needs for data, planning, and resources to address the critical needs for the construction, renovation, operations, and programming of detention facilities in Indian country.
- ***Section 4: Reentry in Tribal Nations***. Tribal Leaders note the importance of including reentry as part of a holistic plan to reduce recidivism and improve community safety by preparing inmates for release. Reentry is a process of assisting offenders in acquiring the life skills needed to succeed in the community upon their release from prison or jail.

The Tribal Justice Plan includes Recommendations at the end of each Section. These Recommendations include short term (six month), mid-term (12 month) and long term goals. DOI, DOJ and the Workgroup have committed to complete the goals in the short and mid- term with existing resources for FY 2011 and FY2012. To accomplish the long term goals, many of the recommendations lay out further action to plan and develop strategies in collaboration with Tribal Leaders and tribal justice officials. This reflects the short timeline to develop this Tribal Justice Plan and the need for additional time to more fully develop long term goals and strategies. To support this planning and collaboration with Tribal Nations, DOI, DOJ and the Workgroup will host further consultations, focus groups and regional meetings with tribes, beginning in late calendar year 2011.

SECTION 2: ALTERNATIVES TO INCARCERATION IN INDIAN COUNTRY

I. Alternatives to Incarceration: An Overview

Alternatives to incarceration are an important part of the American Indian/Alaskan Native (AI/AN) justice system. During the consultation and focus group sessions, participants stated that incarceration should be used as a last resort: although some individuals pose a substantial enough threat to public safety that incarceration is appropriate, most are thought to be in need of community-based alternatives.

Alternatives to incarceration generally include programs, services or supervision that permit an individual to remain within the community, with effective mechanisms in place to ensure public safety. Those convicted of certain drug offenses, for example, may be better served by being ordered to participate in a community-based treatment program or to submit to random urinalysis tests. Without services and treatment options in place to meet offenders' needs in the community, however, judges may have no choice but to sentence an offender to prison or juvenile detention. Some of the benefits of developing and maintaining a meaningful set of incarceration alternatives include:

- Treating the root causes of criminal behavior, such as substance abuse, mental illness, and the impact of victimization, rather than treating only the symptoms of criminal activity.
- Focus on rehabilitation (education, vocational training, and behavioral change) rather than on retribution.

- Keep offenders connected to their families and communities, and support pro-social[12] development.
- Judges may have greater latitude in sentencing decisions if there are viable alternatives to incarceration.
- Conserve resources, both economically and practically; for example, alternative programs can save limited bed space for violent offenders.

Of the over 40 comments received during the release of the draft Plan, over 15 of the comments expressed strong support for the continuation of funding, training and technical assistance to Tribal Nations to plan, implement and enhance Healing to Wellness courts as an alternative to incarceration.

II. Alternatives to Incarceration: Strategies

Developing a system of alternatives is no easy task. It involves identifying the needs of individual communities, securing adequate resources, and developing internal capacity to provide needed supervision and services. Below is a brief summary of strategies, all of which are based on empirical research, that support the use of alternative detention plans in Tribal Nations.

Using Alternatives When They Count the Most

A critical step in developing alternatives is to define the specific Tribal Nation's needs. The National Institute of Corrections (NIC), through the Native American and Alaskan Technical Assistance Project (NAATAP), developed a project guide, *Alternatives to Incarceration of Offenders*, which suggests, among other things, that policies, practices, and programs should be developed for each of the decision points within a criminal justice system.[13] These decision points include the decision to arrest; the decision to refer to pre-trial detention; the decision to prosecute; the decision to release from pre-trial detention; the timeliness and efficiency of the trial process; the timeliness and efficiency of the pre-sentence investigation process; and the management and use of sentence modifications.[14]

By reviewing these decision points, jurisdictions may be able to identify specific interventions to reduce the need for incarceration. These decision points should be considered alongside a jurisdiction's empirical data on arrest numbers, sentencing placements, and violations of release conditions. They should also be considered in connection with community values and culturally- based interventions, as this information may be appropriate for and helpful to individual communities developing alternatives.

Evidence-Based Practice

Criminal justice research in the past few decades suggests that the some of the most effective methods to reduce recidivism are achieved by employing evidence-based practices.[15] When implementing alternatives to incarceration, this means identifying the risk, needs, and responsivity of an individual offender. Evidence-based practices emphasize that certain developmental steps must precede others: for example, offenders must be first assessed for risk and then for need before they can be effectively managed.[16] Areas of inquiry to determine risk and needs include criminal history, substance abuse, past decision-making and peer groups, relationship history, employment and financial history, and housing.

One framework for evidence-based practice is based on a set of interdependent principles, which include assessing the risks and needs of an offender; enhancing motivation for initiating and maintaining behavioral changes (for example, using motivational interview techniques as opposed to persuasion tactics); targeting interventions (for example, prioritizing supervision and treatment resources for higher-risk offenders); employing cognitive behavioral treatment; increasing positive reinforcement; engaging ongoing support in an offender's natural community; measuring the outcome of interventions as well as offender and staff performance; and providing measurable feedback.[17] Given the breadth of these principles, coordination with behavioral health partners such as the Indian Health Service (IHS) and the Substance Abuse and Mental Health Services Administration (SAMHSA) may be critical to successful implementation.

Research is limited on the effectiveness of culturally based strategies to address the needs of tribal members. Tribal Nations should be given the flexibility to employ culturally based strategies to address the needs of each tribal justice system, especially where no evidence based practices exist. At the same time, additional research on the effectiveness of promising practices and tools being employed in Tribal Nations, including Healing to Wellness Courts, would address this gap in knowledge. Notably, a focus group participant from the Chippewa Cree Tribe reported that her community has experienced a significant reduction in recidivism in response to employing evidence-based principles.[18] Over the past two years, the tribe implemented risk and needs assessments for both adult and juvenile offenders, and began using assessment scores to target interventions toward higher-risk individuals.

Law enforcement also used a short, eight-question screening tool to identify an offender's risk of recidivism. Most low-risk persons were generally not detained and few, if any, interventions were employed.

Supervision

In order to develop the most effective continuum of alternatives to incarceration, communities are encouraged to consider establishing supervision services in addition to treatment and programming. Supervision that occurs in the community is often done through the probation/parole or community corrections department[19]. Probation officers in most jurisdictions serve many different roles, and tribal probation officers are no exception. These probation officers are required to both sanction offenders for violating conditions of their probation and to reward those under supervision for positive behavioral change. Probation officers often have high caseloads, multiple responsibilities, and competing demands. In the area of juvenile justice, probation officers may need specialized training on issues such as child development and family engagement. Case management can also assist with these strategies.

In 2010, the American Probation and Parole Association (APPA) published *Tribal Probation: An Overview for Tribal Court Judges,*[20] a guide intended to provide tribal probation personnel with information on administrative screening and assessment tools. These tools can facilitate the development of supervision plans that protect the community and hold the offender accountable, as well as identify more accurately any treatment needs that may be contributing to the offender's criminal behavior.[21] In addition, the development of tribally driven risk assessment tools, or norming of existing tools for a specific tribe should also be explored.

Planning, Funding and Partnerships

These approaches will benefit from planning, using data to define needs and engaging partners to address the range of needs of tribal members under criminal supervision. Another key element is having the foundation of basic court functions for addressing crime in a Tribal Nation, using either traditional methods or a tribal court. Some tribes may not have the resources to fully manage these functions, which are needed to then implement many of the alternatives to incarceration discussed in this Section. At the same time, implementation and sustainment efforts can be complex due to the bifurcation of funding from the federal government. The BIA funds approximately 188 courts via Public Law (P.L.) 93-638 contracts and self-governance compacts, and provides direct services to Courts of Indian Offenses. The BIA also funds start-up costs for tribes implementing new tribal courts. Initial funding to plan, start up, or enhance tribal court and probation functions are also supported through grants, training and technical assistance from the Department of Justice (DOJ). In addition, funding from IHS, SAMHSA, or the Department of Housing and Urban Development (HUD) would need to be leveraged to provide critical services such as medical and behavioral health treatment and transitional housing.

As a result, alternative funding, such as grants, can be uncertain and requires significant planning and coordination. For example, in the 2010 survey of tribal courts, securing funding and sustaining funding were two out of the top three barriers that tribes faced in developing and managing a Healing to Wellness court. It is critical that alternatives be implemented with the key partners in the specific tribes' justice systems, such as law enforcement, courts (judiciary, prosecutors, and defense counsel), probation and pretrial agencies, advocates, victims and family services partners and other service and health providers.

III. Alternative to Incarceration Programs Used in Indian Country

Below are a few examples of programs discussed in focus groups and consultations that suggest promising results. These programs could be used in other jurisdictions, with appropriate modification according to community needs.

- ***Tribal Healing to Wellness Courts.*** These courts, often referred to as "Wellness Courts," provide Tribal Nations with the opportunity to address issues caused by substance abuse and to establish offender accountability through comprehensive supervision, drug testing, treatment services, immediate sanctions and incentives, and case management.[22] This court model has been used with both adult and juvenile offenders.
- ***Juvenile Detention Alternatives Initiative (JDAI)***. An initiative of the Annie E. Casey Foundation, implemented with DOJ, JDAI focuses on the juvenile detention component of the juvenile justice system because youth are often unnecessarily or inappropriately detained at great expense, with long-lasting negative consequences for both

public safety and youth development. JDAI promotes changes to policies, practices, and programs to reduce reliance on secure confinement; improve public safety; reduce racial disparities and bias; save taxpayers' dollars; and stimulate overall juvenile justice reforms. Since its inception in 1992, JDAI has repeatedly demonstrated that jurisdictions can safely reduce reliance on secure detention.

- ***Circles of Care.***[23] The Circles of Care Program provides tribes and urban American Indian organizations with three-year grants to identify and analyze community needs systematically. The grants provide funding to develop culturally appropriate strategies that can be put into action to serve young people with serious behavioral health challenges. Families of these youth also participate in the program. With the help of the entire community, grantees develop models of care, create new partnerships, and position themselves to obtain additional resources to help realize plans for comprehensive and culturally appropriate behavioral health services for children, youth, and families. The grant program currently supports eight tribes and urban Indian organizations across the country: Crow Creek Sioux; Karuk Tribe; the Pueblo of San Felipe; Standing Rock Sioux Tribe; Mashantucket Pequot Tribal Nation; American Indian Center of Chicago, Illinois; and the Indian Center in Lincoln, Nebraska.
- ***The Circle Project.***[24] *The Circle Project was an initiative of DOJ that provided incentives to help tribes bring the individual components of their justice systems together to address crime and social problems. Three tribes –Pueblo of Zuni, Northern Cheyenne, and Oglala Sioux - participated in the project. One tribe reported a 40 percent drop in alcohol- related crime and simple assault from 2001-2004.*
- ***Peacemaker Courts.***[25] Navajo judges revived traditional peacemaking in 1982 by creating the Navajo Peacemaker Court, described as a "modern Navajo institution that is based on the traditional forum for dispute resolution."[26] The peacemaking process includes discussion and consensus decision-making. All participants are treated as equals with the purpose of preserving ongoing relationships and restoring disputants to a state of balance, harmony, and peace with each other as well as their families and communities.[27] Peacemaking courts may not be appropriate for many violent crimes, particularly domestic violence and sexual assault. Other tribes may want to explore models, like peacemaking, that build upon local traditions.

- ***Anchorage Youth Courts.*** The Anchorage Youth Court (AYC) began in 1989 to "stop illegal behavior while encouraging understanding and respect for the law through positive peer pressure in a formal court setting."[28] The AYC provides formal legal training, a youth court bar association, and a juvenile diversion court operated completely by youth in grades seven to twelve, with adults serving as advisors. The State of Alaska Juvenile Justice Division refers cases of youth ages 12 to 18, arrested for committing a criminal offense, but not considered a threat to themselves or society to the AYC. Between 1989 and 2006, 4,237 juvenile criminal (delinquency) cases were sent to AYC for adjudication. In this same period, juveniles paid over $79,000 in victim restitution and worked over 101,000 community service hours.[29]

IV. RECOMMENDATIONS: ACTIONS AND STRATEGIES

Foundational Elements of a Tribal Justice Program

- **Develop a system of alternatives to incarceration.** Building upon the strategies listed in this Section, Tribal Nations can develop community supervision and service options to provide alternatives to institutional confinement. Tribes can also identify those points in the system where incarceration occurs, examine the reasons why, and explore alternative strategies to monitor safely the offender in the community.
- **Make interventions culturally specific to meet the needs of individual communities.** As described above, tribes should identify and prioritize their needs, develop political support, gather diverse stakeholders, use data to inform decision-making, and develop an action plan. Tribes should explore and expand the use of traditional approaches such as Peacemaking Courts and Healing to Wellness Courts, and community courts. Tribes should also engage tribal elders, leaders, and community residents in planning and executing alternative programs. Due to the lack of research on Indian country specific evidence based models, more research should be conducted of tribally driven practices such as Healing to Wellness Courts.
- **Encourage intra-governmental cooperation.** Determination of criminal jurisdiction in Indian country depends on several factors,

including the nature of the crime; whether the alleged offender, victim, or both are Indian or non-Indian; and whether a treaty or federal statute has conferred jurisdiction on a particular government. In certain areas of Indian country, states have acquired jurisdiction over specified crimes committed by or against Indians pursuant to Public Law 280. This jurisdictional complexity requires collaboration and cooperation across governments. For example, tribes in Public Law 280 jurisdictions could consider presenting to state officials alternatives to detention for one or more primary criminal offenses (e.g., drug possession or driving while under the influence).

- **Explore electronic monitoring as an alternative to incarceration.** Electronic monitoring options—including monitoring for location (home/school/confinement) or alcohol abuse—could be a valuable option for providing the least restrictive and appropriate environment for many offenders. This option could also keep offenders connected to their family, community, and culture, and could be used with both adults and juveniles. "Central check-in" options for alcohol monitoring bracelets that require the offender to check-in daily at a designated location instead of requiring specific equipment in the offender's home can also facilitate the offender's regular contact with support and treatment services.
- **Explore the feasibility of work release through tribal jails in place of federal halfway houses, including any potential impact of such a program on victims of crime.** Work release programs through tribal jails are an alternative to federal halfway houses. These programs can help to reduce recidivism and to improve individual offenders' quality of life within their families and communities.
- **Explore enhanced resources for community corrections and supervision.** Tribes seek federal help to build and enhance tribal probation activities to allow for community- based supervision and programming, rather than detention, for mid-risk offenders. Through the Bureau of Justice Assistance's (BJA's) Correctional Systems and Correctional Alternatives on Tribal Lands (CSCATL), and BJA's Tribal Courts Assistance Programs (TCAP), tribes can engage in strategic planning and obtain training to plan, build, and enhance community supervision strategies. Moreover, the Bureau of Indian Affairs (BIA) provides training on community corrections and supervision.

- **Explore the use of community service as part of alternatives.** Community service as part of the sentencing terms can offer opportunities for tribal members to assist their tribes as a consequence of the crime, build new skills and work experience, and to instill pride in contributing to their tribes. Tribal members should be engaged in identifying and implementing these service opportunities.
- **Increase access to after school and summer programs for youth.** Many tribes do not have options for after school or summer activities for their youth. Whether cultural, recreational, community-oriented, or academic, these activities have positive effects on academic success, social behavior, and intellectual development, and can serve as an important prevention strategy. The Bureau of Indian Education (BIE) and the Substance Abuse and Mental Health Services Administration (SAMHSA) are working together to implement the portions of TLOA relating to summer programs for youth.
- **Increase access to other critical support services.** Assess and increase access to critical supports such as transportation for largely rural Tribal Nations to ensure transportation to critical prevention and community based programs for tribal members at risk for involvement in crime. In addition, increase options for transitional housing for juvenile and adult participants in alternatives to incarceration to ensure access to a sober and safe environment.

Short term resources that federal agencies will make available (within six months):

- DOJ's TCAP and Indian Alcohol and Substance Abuse Assistance (IASAP) and Tribal Youth Programs (TYP) will help Tribal Nations assess their needs and plan community- based alternatives to incarceration, including tribal courts, probation, after school programming and diversion programs.
- DOJ's TCAP, IASAP and Drug Courts programs will support the creation of Healing to Wellness Courts, Peacemaker Courts, and Community Courts.
- DOJ's TCAP and IASAP and Drug Courts programs will support the creation and enhancement of tribal probation agencies.
- DOI will continue to promote tribal self determination for tribal corrections via P.L. 93 638 contracts and self-governance compacts.

condition,"[31] plagued by overcrowding and serious disrepair. Many lack sufficient staffing, training and funding to function safely and effectively.[32] Given these limitations, some tribes would like to build multi-justice centers where law enforcement, courts, corrections and community services, including community supervision, treatment and programming can be coordinated and leveraged effectively.

The federal partners play a vital role in improving corrections systems, including facilities, in Indian country. Their ongoing collaboration and communication with tribes will help tribes better understand and access federal programs, processes and funding. In particular, tribes have expressed a strong desire for greater coordination between DOJ and DOI with respect to awards for grants that may be used to construct tribal detention facilities (which may be provided by DOJ) and P.L. 93-638 contracts and self-governance compacts for funding operations (provided by DOI). The Departments are committed to coordinating to address this and other issues related to detention in Indian country. This Section addresses the construction, operation, and maintenance of juvenile and adult detention facilities (including regional facilities); contracting with state and local detention facilities; and the construction of federal detention facilities in Indian country.

I. Federal Funding for Tribal Detention

The earliest federally funded jails in Indian country were built in the late 1960s with funding from DOJ's Law Enforcement Assistance Administration (LEAA).[33] In the mid-1970s DOI also funded tribal jails through the BIA. Since then, tribes have increasingly used incarceration as an option to address growing public safety issues. Currently, several federal funding streams support tribal detention facilities:

- ***Correctional Systems and Correctional Alternatives on Tribal Lands (CSCATL) for Construction***. Since 1999 the DOJ's Office of Justice Programs (OJP) and Bureau of Justice Assistance (BJA)[34] have been administering the CSCATL[35] program, which authorized funding only for the "bricks and mortar" construction costs of adult and juvenile correctional facilities, including planning, renovating and constructing, but not for operations or maintenance costs.
- ***Expansion of CSCATL under American Recovery and Reinvestment Act of 2009 (Recovery Act) and TLOA for Construction.*** Under the

Recovery Act and more recently under TLOA, the scope of funding has been increased to authorize the planning, renovation and construction of multi-purpose justice centers and alternatives to incarceration. To date, DOJ has provided funding for the construction of 35 new correctional or correctional alternative facilities and awarded an additional 39 grants to tribes to renovate or complete existing facilities, including a number of awards to help tribes comply with provisions for "sight and sound"[36] separation of juveniles from adult inmates. DOJ also provides training and technical assistance to assist tribes with planning, construction and renovation.

- ***Funding for Operations and Management through BIA***. The BIA is the federal agency with the main responsibility for overseeing and/or operating adult and juvenile facilities in Indian country. It manages or oversees detention facilities that are (1) operated by the BIA; (2) contracted with tribes under the provisions of Pub. L. 93-638;[37] (3) self-governance compacted between BIA and the tribes; or (4) operated by state and local entities under contract with the BIA. A small number of Indian country jails are operated strictly by tribes without BIA fiscal support. In FY 2011 the BIA funded 83 corrections programs providing support for 69 detention facilities in 54 Tribal Nations. These funds support operation and management costs such as utilities, staff, janitorial service and refuse collection. The BIA also funds contract bed space in state and local facilities when applicable to meet program needs where beds in tribal jails are not available.
- ***Funding for Construction and Repair of BIA Facilities.*** Facilities maintenance for detention facilities was previously included in the Public Safety and Justice Construction budget within Construction, as part of the Indian Affairs budget at DOI. Starting in FY 2012, facilities maintenance funding for detention facilities will be included in the Public Safety and Justice budget within the Operation of Indian Programs account.
- ***Operations Funding for New CSCATL Facilities through BIA and Indian Affairs.*** BIA issues certificates of occupancy for new CSCATL funded facilities but distributes funds based on availability. Indian Affairs funds operations at varying levels, but generally does not fund any program in full. Tribes that can afford to supplement BIA funding generally have superior facilities, which provide programming, education, treatment and other services for adult and juvenile offenders.

- ***Programmatic Funding for Tribal Facilities.*** Resources for programming are leveraged through partnerships with social service and behavioral health agencies such as the Indian Health Service (IHS), Bureau of Indian Education (BIE) and state and county agencies and non-profits.

Because of the bifurcated funding streams, DOJ provides a list of CSCATL applicants to BIA to get recommendations on how to prioritize the funding requests and coordinates project management through quarterly conference calls.

II. Assessing and Planning for Correctional Needs

DOJ helps tribes assess their correctional needs as a first step to exploring the construction of facilities, either through a planning grant or training and technical assistance. This process, initially called the PONI[38] (Planning of New Institutions) and now the PACIFIC (Planning Alternatives and Correctional Institutions For Indian Country) training, helps tribes conduct a communitywide assessment for the purpose of developing a comprehensive master plan for the design, use, capacity, and cost of adult and juvenile justice sanctions and services. Through this process, the tribe can then explore an array of options, including prototypical designs for local correctional facilities, multiservice centers, and regional facilities, as well as community-based alternatives to ease jail overcrowding.

III. Facility Planning Challenges

Some tribes are renovating their facilities, others are expanding, and others are planning new facilities. Each stage entails many decisions related to identifying the purpose of the facility and community expectations, funding, staffing, training, facility usage and functions, maintenance, and operations and management. The following sections discuss the challenges present at each stage of the process.

Complexity of Detention Center Planning Projects

Facility planning projects in non-tribal communities can take between four and six years to complete; in Indian country, projects can take even longer due to the challenges of jurisdiction, geography and governance. If a project is to be successful, Tribal Leaders must support it, and the tribe must have accurate data about crime, arrests, bookings, and average daily jail population in order to plan for capacity needs. These data are often scattered among different agencies and may not be automated, nor have the proper protections in place for juvenile offender information. With the exception of data collected directly by tribal justice agencies, it is often impossible to determine the number of AI/AN within an aggregated number or crime statistic.

Significant Data Needs and Limited Automation

Three types of data are typically collected during the needs assessment and pre-design phases:

- ***Historical Trend Analysis:*** An analysis of types of crime, crimes reported, arrests, detention bookings, average daily population, case filings and dispositions.
- ***Inmate Profile Analysis:*** An analysis of inmate demographics, criminal offenses, rate of release, residence, and classification information to inform facility usage, target groups, needed programs and sentencing.
- ***Population Projections:*** A baseline forecast to show the implications of current use patterns on future capacity requirements, and scenarios which estimate the impact of potential alternatives that are created.

Although some of this information may be available to a tribe, obtaining it may be complicated by jurisdictional issues and a lack of automation. Manual systems can be vulnerable to missing and inaccurate data. Detention operational data such as average daily population, seasonal trends, behavior in the facility, classification interviews/scoring about security levels of the population and inmate needs, health contacts, visiting levels and cost and revenue elements are even less likely to exist. Tribes need help to build and enhance data collection and extraction capacity.

Collaboration with Many Agencies

In Indian country, many agencies may need to be involved in planning tribal correctional facilities and multi-purpose justice centers, including the state police, local law enforcement, federal law enforcement agencies,[39] tribal prosecutor, tribal court, the county sheriff, county prosecutor, county and state court, the U.S. Attorney, the federal District Court, and the state department of corrections and community corrections. All of these agencies may have a role to play in tribal justice functions and having the support of these agencies can reduce barriers, increase resources and support and ensure that all aspects of jurisdiction and key incarceration functions are addressed in planning a facility. Federal agencies like BJA, BIA, BIE, IHS, the Office of Juvenile Justice and Delinquency Prevention (OJJDP) and the Substance Abuse and Mental Health Services Administration (SAMHSA) should support the planning process when substance abuse, courts, corrections and juvenile justice issues arise. DOJ offers training and technical assistance to support intergovernmental collaboration in strategic planning, law enforcement, detention, and courts.

Developing a Coordinated Approach to Facility Usage

The relationship of substance abuse to crime in Indian country is well documented. Planning for facility space to support holistic approaches to address co-occurring substance abuse, mental health and health issues in jails will require the collaboration of behavioral health and justice systems in order to reduce recidivism and improve public safety.

New programs and services will be needed if jails are to implement the longer sentences authorized under TLOA's enhanced sentencing authority, yet some facilities in Indian country do not have classification systems to determine the security levels for prisoners. Indian country facilities often lack services or programming for longer-term adults and juveniles and are unequipped to treat the conditions which led to incarceration, increasing the likelihood that released offenders will reoffend.

Projecting and Managing Costs

For every dollar that is spent building the structure, between nine and 15 dollars are spent to operate it.[40] Operations costs include staffing, supplies and maintenance, but 80 percent of operational costs are staffing.[41] Because staffing is dependent upon facility design, jurisdictions must identify staffing requirements during the planning stages rather than wait until the building is open.

Tribes also need to balance their options for size and quality of new facilities with available funding. Planning, design and construction grant funding levels do not always fully fund project costs. Some tribes with strong economies or enterprise revenues may be able fund a portion of the construction costs, but most must coordinate multiple funding streams to support a building project, a challenging prospect due to multiple reporting requirements and timelines. Funds must also be allocated for transition planning, before the facility opens. In addition to "academy" or pre-service training and orientation needed for new employees, transition planning requires training on the facility and its operations, policies and procedures; post training; simulation training; and inmate orientation. To accomplish these goals, some facilities have hired a transition coordinator to develop policies and procedures and hire and train staff while the facility is under construction.

A process should also be developed to fund activation and start-up costs for detention centers that will be operated by the BIA or tribes. This activation and start-up funding must cover the period prior to and during activation and must include a reasonable time-period for the BIA to develop and receive appropriations for the facility.

Regionalization and Contracting with State and Local Partners

Regional detention facilities are those operated under a joint agreement between two or more tribal (or state or local) governments, with representatives of the participating jurisdictions having varying authority over policy, budget, operations, and personnel.[42] Regional facilities may offer a viable way to reduce costs and may make it easier to implement a wider range of consistent programming and to coordinate with services offered regionally by IHS. On the other hand, regional facilities may be located far from a prisoner's tribe or home, making it difficult for families to visit or to participate in rehabilitation services or to coordinate with tribal justice representatives on programming, rehabilitation support and reentry planning.

Another option is for tribes to contract for beds in state or local facilities, but this arrangement poses the same challenges for programming as regionalization when the prisoner is far from home, even if these types of facilities have more resources to provide programs and services than are available in Indian country facilities. The use of contracted facilities can also create logistical issues for court hearings, medical needs, and other programs and services, requiring extensive coordination for transportation.

Placing Federal Facilities in Indian Country

Federal resources for detention in Indian country should be focused in BIA and BJA to address the needs of Tribal Nations. As discussed in Section Four, it is also recommended that there be further exploration of another option: the use of tribal corrections agencies as contractors for halfway houses for transitioning federal inmates. Although the Federal Bureau of Prisons (BOP) is one of the leading agencies building correctional and detention

Cross Cutting Issues: Resources, Staffing and Training

Most tribes have limited federal and tribal resources to build facilities and to create, enhance and manage their tribal safety strategies. This challenge can be exacerbated by the lack of coordination between federal and state agencies about tribal resources such as funding, training and technical assistance. During the focus groups and consultations, tribal leadership spoke of the need for significant enhancement in training assistance and resources as well as strategies to recruit and retain qualified staff. Training should include basic and ongoing skills training for staff as well as leadership and management training for tribal justice officials overseeing agency level work. In addition, training should include mentoring by other tribal justice officials with experience in planning, building and operating tribal corrections agencies and facilities. Strategies include increased training and collaboration with state and federal training resources, a streamlined hiring process, and enhanced infrastructure for staff in tribal communities, such as housing.

VI. Detention Programs being Used in Indian Country

Multipurpose Justice Center

The Shoshone-Bannock Tribes' multi-purpose center in Idaho houses an adult jail (80 beds), and a juvenile detention center (20 beds), which include: a medical examination room; a classroom; dayrooms; office space; a multi-purpose room; visitation area; and a dedicated outdoor recreation area. In addition to these detention functions, the center also houses a courtroom, court offices, the police station, dispatch and other law enforcement functions.

Regional Facilities and Contracting

The Ute Mountain Ute Tribe operates a direct service program which houses adult and juvenile offenders from a number of reservations.

The Hualapai Juvenile Detention and Rehabilitation Center in Arizona, a juvenile facility, accepts referrals from BIA for juveniles from other tribes.

In Nebraska, the Omaha, Winnebago, and Ponca Tribes and Santee Sioux Nation are working cooperatively to develop a regional Adult Multi-Justice Center and a Juvenile Multi-Justice Center.

In Nevada, the Reno-Sparks Indian Colony, Fallon Paiute Shoshone Tribe and other Nevada tribes have been discussing the formation of a Regional Tribal Justice Facility through the Inter- Tribal Council of Nevada.

The Sault Tribe of Chippewa (Sault Ste. Marie), Michigan juvenile facility is licensed by the State of Michigan, providing contract beds to neighboring communities.

Use of Cultural Elements in Building

The Salt River Pima-Maricopa Indian Community Adult and Juvenile Detention Center in Arizona constructed a 130 person correctional facility with a curved front wall, designed to reflect cultural and community values, and focuses on rehabilitation and successful reintegration of its members back into the community as part of the healing process.

The Northern Cheyenne Tribe in Montana integrated an array of services under one roof: cultural aspects are expressed in traditional two and three-dimensional forms and decorative elements using indigenous materials and colors.

The Sac and Fox Nation in Oklahoma constructed a regional juvenile detention facility and multi-justice center with tribal cultural healing practices in mind. The facility design incorporated movement from east to west, talking circles, and outdoor protected locations for traditional healing, and indoor sanctuaries for multi-dimensional practices.

VII. Recommendations

Planning Recommendations

- ***Assess Needs and Collect Data to Inform Planning***. Tribes may wish to engage in structured justice system planning efforts to determine justice system needs. A system- wide assessment will enable tribes to determine the source of justice systems needs, such as inmate populations, offenses, and other factors. Create long term strategies that enhance the capacity to define system requirements, share data and employ analytical tools to link federal, tribal and state information systems that support management and budget forecasting in tribal justice systems. Support research to identify effective methods in Tribal Nations.
- ***Support Implementation of Jail Standards.*** Use the range of existing jail standards to comply with applicable case law and construction techniques that will result in safe and secure confinement and operations. Standards can ensure effective implementation of inmate classification, security and safety of staff and prisoners, health

services, sanitation, preventative maintenance, discipline, grievance procedures, exercise, education, offender services and activities, as well as qualifications and training requirements for staff.

- ***Intergovernmental and Multidisciplinary Coordination.*** Broad-based partnerships involving key federal, tribal, state and local partners can build stronger, more sustainable programs. These collaborations can address challenges related to jurisdiction over tribal members and increasing the use of tribally based correctional interventions in the areas of alternatives, incarceration and reentry planning. These efforts should also include multi disciplinary teams that reflect the range of issues facing the criminogenic needs of detainees and those incarcerated. The teams should include corrections and pretrial, law enforcement, courts (judiciary, prosecution, defense and administrators), public and behavioral health (including sexual assault nurse examiners), education, victim service providers and community and family supports.
- ***Juvenile Detention and Treatment.*** Assess needs for juvenile detention and conduct inventory of existing funding and technical assistance resources dedicated to tribal youth across federal agencies. Develop a training program for peer and adult advocates in juvenile detention facilities in Indian country. Establish community and tribal specific coalitions to advise and support the tribal juvenile detention facilities.
- ***Regionalization and Contracting.*** Support tribes seeking to explore the use of tribally driven regional approaches and partnerships with state and local partners for contracting of bed space to enhance efficiency and sustainability. Determine bed space needs, including populations, security level and length of stay, and develop short- and long-term capacity plans to optimize currently available beds.

Operations and Programming Recommendations

- ***Operations.*** Establish baseline standards for funding facility operations in Indian country. Develop strategies to adjust funding based upon the economy, including funding for 638 contracts, self-governance compacts and direct service funding.
- ***Develop Data-driven, Comprehensive Programming.*** Tribal corrections agencies should use planning data and validated, tribally normed risk assessment tools to assess key trends in their jail population. From this data, tribal justice agencies should define and

create a comprehensive plan to provide critical programming, including treatment, in behavioral and public health, education, employment, life skills and family supports, to address criminogenic needs and reduce the risk of recidivism. In program implementation, data should be collected and used to enhance program management for corrections and reentry.

- ***Collaborate with BOP and BIA Facilities for High-Risk Offenders.*** Some prisoners from Tribal Nations require significant security or specialized programming that can be offered at larger BOP and BIA facilities. Tribal Nations may wish to collaborate with BOP and BIA to enhance the availability and use of these resources and better plan and coordinate reentry activities.
- ***Special Populations:*** Develop procedures and policies to address special populations such as females; juveniles; and geriatric prisoners.

VIII. Construction and Maintenance Recommendations

- ***Facility Construction and Maintenance.*** Despite the progress made with DOJ funding, some tribal detention facilities are in disrepair. All tribal detention facilities should meet the recently released BIA jail standards for building specifications and should plan for maintenance and infrastructure needs. Tribal corrections would benefit from project management support during planning, design, construction and renovation to ensure access to technical expertise.
- ***Transition Support Strategies.*** To ensure the smooth opening of a newly constructed or renovated facility, significant planning is needed. Requests for operational funding should be made before construction is authorized to ensure staff are available when the facility is ready for occupancy. Resources, training and technical assistance are also needed prior to opening the facility.
- ***Develop Multilevel Funding Approaches.*** Coordinate and assist tribes with leveraging funding from multiple governmental and non-governmental sources to support tribal detention construction, maintenance and renovation. Enhance training, technical assistance and collaboration efforts at the intergovernmental and tribal levels.
- ***Peer-to-Peer Support.*** Continue to support networking and peer-to-peer support opportunities for tribes to exchange information on successes, challenges and pitfalls to avoid in detention facility

construction projects and assistance for tribal justice officials in their leadership roles.

Short term resources that federal agencies will make available (within six months):

- DOJ's CSCATL program will offer training and technical assistance to interested tribes to support assessment of corrections needs; development of master plans to address tribal justice system needs; project management; strategies for corrections, alternatives to detention and multi-purpose justice facilities; and support for consortia of tribes to build regional facilities. DOJ's National Field-Generated program will offer training, technical assistance and grant funding to support strategies for the prevention, victim response and prosecution of sexual assaults against prisoners in tribal correctional facilities.
- DOJ's Tribal Juvenile Detention and Reentry Green Demonstration Program will offer training and technical assistance to support this work with Juvenile Detention. Funding from DOJ, BIA, USDA, HUD and IHS will support grants, training, technical assistance and project management to tribes building facilities. BIA can support funding, training, and technical assistance to tribes maintaining facilities.
- DOI will continue to promote tribal self-determination and self-governance for tribal corrections via 638 contracts and self-governance compacts.
- DOJ's Work Group on Intergovernmental Collaboration will continue to assess and implement strategies to support intergovernmental collaboration with federal, tribal, and state agencies. DOJ has several programs to support intergovernmental collaboration in tribal justice.
- DOI, DOJ and the Work Group will sponsor several regional meetings in 2011 to collaborate with Tribal Nations in implementing the recommendations in the Tribal Justice Plan.
- The Work Group will explore strategies to support hiring, basic competency training and obtaining security clearances, identifying ways to streamline these processes.

Mid-term resources that federal agencies will make available (within twelve months):

- The Work Group will develop and enhance collaborative strategies to increase the accessibility of federal funding and resources for Tribal Nations in the areas of alternatives, detention, and reentry.
- The Work Group will explore options and potential resources to promote comprehensive programming for detention facilities. Strong multi-disciplinary collaboration is necessary to leverage resources for good detention programming. Federal agencies can play a leadership role in supporting the collaboration at the tribal level, given the range of roles on the federal, tribal, state and local levels.
- The Work Group should identify existing funding, training and technical assistance that supports detention and reentry, and make it available in a central location online.
- DOI and DOJ will enhance their current coordination and planning efforts related to funding new construction, to maximize success of these projects.
- DOI will explore the mechanisms for funding the operations and maintenance of regional facilities which are operated by a non-profit organization on behalf of several tribes, including whether DOI can contract with the non-profit organization (as opposed to with a tribe or tribal organization).
- The Work Group, with BOP and FPS as critical partners, will explore options and potential resources to assist in enhancing identification and provision of services to high risk offenders or those needing specialized services, including sex offenders.
- Provide additional exposure and information regarding the creation of the BOP pilot program under TLOA to house offenders sentenced in tribal courts under the enhanced sentencing authority.

Over the Long Term, if additional resources become available, it is also recommended that:

- Develop, with DOI and DOJ as critical partners, tools to support objective assessment of overall needs and projected costs for planning, building and maintaining tribal corrections, alternatives to detention, and multi-purpose justice facilities and to connect current resources from the various agencies. This should include strategies to

BIA will share information about electronic monitoring bracelets with tribal courts.

- The Bureau of Indian Education (BIE) will make funding available to eligible tribes through Title IV of the Elementary and Secondary Education Act, Pub. L. 89-10, 20 U.S.C. § 70, Part A, 21st Century Schools, for summer youth programs and afterschool programs, and Part B, Safe and Drug Free Schools for anti-drug programs.
- The Work Group will add other critical federal partners to support implementation of the Tribal Justice Plan, including agencies representing civil rights, victims, youth issues, family violence and defense.

Mid-term resources that federal agencies will make available (within twelve months):

- Provide integrated tools and training to identify and educate tribes on multiple funding streams that can be leveraged to build a comprehensive approach to tribal justice. Examples of these funds and tools include TCAP, IASAP, TYP, DOJ's Tribal Juvenile Accountability Discretionary Grant Program, Indian Health Services, Circles of Care and other SAMSHA resources and P.L. 93-638 contracts and self-governance compacts.
- The Work Group will collaborate with the Bureau of Prisons (BOP), the U.S. Probation and Pretrial Service Systems, and the Executive Office for United States Attorneys (EOUSA) to explore the feasibility of a work release program for tribal members who are returning from federal incarceration, which potentially includes funding to support these activities.
- DOJ will fund Tribal Probation Academies in FY 2011 and explore expanded assistance such as training for supervisors and training on planning and managing a tribal probation agency.
- DOJ and DOI, in coordination with other federal agencies, will expand the Juvenile Detention Alternatives Initiative (JDAI) to Indian country.
- DOJ will conduct an initial assessment of witness intimidation in tribal justice systems.

Over the Long Term, if additional resources become available, it is also recommended that:

- Grant funding and flexibility for training, technical assistance, and publications be increased to help tribes plan, build and enhance tribal probation agencies, risk assessment tools and processes, electronic monitoring, and work release programs. This training should include continuing education for staff as well as start up training.
- Grant funding and flexibility be increased for alternatives to incarceration in tribal justice systems.
- Federal training and technical assistance (TTA) specific to capacity-building around TLOA-enhanced sentencing authority and other provisions be created.
- Develop, in coordination with tribes, research knowledge and publications about effective practices in alternatives to incarceration in Indian country.
- DOJ, in coordination with other federal agencies, should develop strategies for juvenile supervision and specialized training for juvenile probation officers.
- Youth-based substance abuse treatment, community-based shelters and group homes, alternative education programs, job training, employment, and parenting classes, be increased, as they are unavailable in Tribal Nations due to a lack of funding and capacity to sustain such programs.

SECTION 3: DETENTION IN INDIAN COUNTRY

As described earlier, many Tribal Leaders expressed a strong belief that incarceration should be a last resort and that tribes should build holistic, community-based alternatives to incarceration. At the same time, Tribal Leaders and tribal justice professionals acknowledge that detention is sometimes necessary. A focus of the Tribal Justice Plan, therefore, is development of a continuum of the best community-based interventions and institutional placement for individual offenders.

Many Tribal Nations do not have the resources to develop a robust and coordinated correctional infrastructure. Many jails in Indian country have not been upgraded since they were built in the 1960s and 1970s.[30] A 2011 evaluation by the Office of the Inspector General (OIG) of the Department of the Interior (DOI) found that many tribal jails remain in “egregious physical

I. Reentry Data

AI/AN adults and juvenile offenders serve short- and long-term sentences or commitments in jails and prisons that are located on and off Indian country and operated by federal, tribal, state, and local authorities. Where an AI/AN person is detained often depends on where the crime occurred, jurisdictional authority, the seriousness of the crime committed, whether the victim and perpetrators are tribal members, and the availability of confinement facilities. In 2009, of the 29,400 confined Indian offenders, most were held in off-reservation jails (9,400, 32 percent) or state prisons or facilities (14,646, 50 percent). Federal prisons held 3,154 Indian prisoners, representing 11 percent of the total Indian people confined in midyear 2009.[54]

Since the majority of AI/AN offenders serve sentences and juvenile commitments in correctional facilities not in Indian country, it is even more critical for tribes to have reentry programs that can prepare these ex-offenders for their return to the community. Within correctional facilities where long-term stays are most likely to occur, the programming opportunities are usually greater than those found in county jails, tribal jails and BIA jails located in Indian country; however, it is even more unlikely that culturally developed programming for AI/AN is provided. As noted in a recent report by the Urban Institute, "a critical challenge in handling youth in the federal system is the lack of residential facilities close to the communities of the offenders," and "such distances likely hamper sustained contact with vital social supports necessary for successful transition back to the community once confinement ends."[55]

II. Challenges in Short-Term (Jail) Reentry

System Challenges

While some jails and detention centers are located in Indian country, most commitments are served in off-reservation jails. Of the 565 federally recognized Indian tribes, only 80 have jails or detention facilities in their communities, however, the implications of P.L. 280, as discussed in Section One and elsewhere in this document, must be considered in determining the potential universe of Indian country jails.[56] In midyear 2009 these tribal facilities held 2,176 Indian people representing seven percent of 29,400 Indian people confined in a correctional facility, both pre-trial and post conviction. Approximately 72 percent were adult males (n=1,571), 16 percent were adult enhance information sharing between federal, tribal and state partners. These efforts should be coordinated with existing efforts and tools.

- Explore, with DOI and DOJ as critical partners, expanded strategies and resources to support the operations, programming, transition and maintenance of detention facilities, such as funding flexibilities, model agreements, market analysis, and studies of feasibility.
- The Work Group review existing screening and assessment tools and develop culturally relevant tools that work for AI/AN populations in developing detention programming. Develop a strategy on long term sustainment of tribal justice systems, programs and regional approaches, including identification of demonstration and long term funding streams and gaps.
- DOI and DOJ should explore strategies to enhance compliance with jail standards.
- DOJ, BIA, and IHS should take the lead in developing a plan to create a peer advocate training program to allow these agencies to serve the most important aspects and greatest needs of juvenile detention facilities in Indian country.

SECTION 4: REENTRY IN TRIBAL NATIONS

Introduction

Reentry is a process of using "programs targeted at promoting the effective reintegration of offenders back to communities upon release from prison and jail," which "is intended to assist offenders in acquiring the life skills needed to succeed in the community and become law abiding citizens."[51] Tribes have always had mechanisms to maintain peace, law, and order; to resolve disputes and conflicts between community members; and to correct those who violate community laws and mores.[52] Tribes continue to build upon cultural strengths and indigenous approaches to create responsive systems to address crime, violence, and victimization problems. While acknowledging that reentry should begin in jails or prisons, successful strategies also depend on community-based supports that include family, community, and tribal government support systems. As noted by a tribal member during the TLOA focus group meetings, "We do not throw away our tribal members[53]."

females (n=348), eight percent were juvenile males (n=183), and three percent juvenile females (n=74)[57].

The multipurpose use of jails affects their ability to provide programs and services and develop reentry plans. Jails typically house both adjudicated and non-adjudicated inmates. Within tribal jails, the average length of stay is five and a half days. Short jail stays present both an opportunity for early intervention and challenges in connecting the inmate with services to aid reentry. Program services can address long-term needs such as substance abuse, co-occurring and mental health disorders, and sex offender treatment. For adults, identification and coordination with good alternatives to incarceration, such as peacemaker courts and community courts for low-risk offenders, and Healing to Wellness courts and monitoring tools with supervision for mid- to high-risk offenders, can help address the factors driving recidivism.

Juvenile Detention Center (JDC) system and policy changes enhance resources for restorative practices programs and family and community engagement at each stage of detention, from placement to reentry, through coordinated support of federal, tribal, state and local partners. Juvenile reentry requires working with local schools and families to help youth transition back into school and home.

Tribes that do not have jails contract with other facilities for adult and/or juvenile offenders. These facilities are sometimes located far away on other tribes' reservations or in cities. The long distances present problems in maintaining staff and family contact, which hinders participation in rehabilitation efforts and developing reentry plans. Once offenders are transferred to off-reservation jails, tribal justice agencies have no control over the treatment and services they receive. Together, these issues hinder effective reentry planning for adults and juveniles.

Data, Infrastructure, and Program Challenges

Jail is often the first opportunity for offenders to be assessed to identify their criminogenic needs.[58] Unfortunately, jails in general have limited capacity to provide individualized assessments and programming. As a result, problems persist and some individuals may reoffend due to inadequate reentry support to address ongoing criminogenic needs such as substance abuse, mental illness and unemployment. Evidence-based services including assessing need and offering prerelease and community-based interventions can prevent reoffending. These evidence-based practices should be flexible enough to incorporate each tribe's cultural values and history, and more research should be conducted on the effectiveness of traditional approaches to reentry. These should be developed for adult, juvenile and specific gender populations. The alternatives to incarceration discussed in Section Two will be critical elements of the reentry response for those jail populations.

An important role for tribal justice systems is to support and develop community-based resources and programming for ex-offenders and their families. To ensure that reentry programming and planning is culturally responsive, Tribal Leaders may need to negotiate intergovernmental agreements with state, municipal or county jails.[59] To assist in this effort, tribes may benefit from training and technical assistance to support information sharing, analysis, and collaboration.

Tribes are especially challenged by the breadth and depth of services needed by reentering youth. Many of these needs apply to adult offenders as well. These include behavioral health needs such as suicide prevention and access to psychiatric medications; substance abuse treatment and mental health services; educational programming that addresses preexisting issues such as learning disabilities, school failure, truancy, and drop-out status; assistance to repair disrupted family relationships and dysfunctional family situations; reconnection to cultural and spiritual practices needed for well-being and emotional health; access to victim services to address victimization in past or exposure to violence and career preparation or training. There is a need for more federal funding and a coordinated federal approach to child, youth and family needs in Indian country.

Tribal Nations would benefit from an overall framework that aligns tribal youth policies across federal agencies in accordance with relevant provisions of TLOA. The Juvenile Justice and Delinquency Prevention Act as amended (JJDPA), Pub. L. 103-227, Title II, Part B, stipulates that states in their three-year plans must include the juvenile justice needs of tribes. Federal partners can assist in the coordination of federal funding resources to tribal JDCs for education, behavioral health, and vocational training services to enhance academic success and pro-social behavior for detained and reentering AI/AN youth. These efforts should be coordinated between DOJ, BIA, Indian Health Service (IHS), the Bureau of Indian Education (BIE), and community providers who offer essential educational and behavioral health services for youth, including detention.

Challenges in Engaging Community and Family

Offenders are often out of touch with the effects of their actions and incarceration on their families. Additionally, there are limited resources that focus on establishing culture-based conflict resolution or peacekeeping systems that can help offenders apologize to victims and families, make amends or reparation, and regain trust. Facility staff may be reluctant or not know how to work with tribal officials who can support victim-offender mediation where it is appropriate or agreeable with victims. Research has shown that children may benefit from maintaining healthy relationships with their incarcerated parents. Strong parent-child relationships may aid in children's adjustment to their parents' incarceration and help to mitigate many of the negative outcomes for children that are associated with parental incarceration. Maintaining contact also helps the incarcerated parent by improving the reentry process and reducing recidivism, which would likely benefit the child.

Incarcerated youth may not have a positive relationship with a caring adult in their family or community. Many families need guidance and some need intervention regarding parenting skills, housing and economic resources support, and information on impact of victimization or exposure to violence. For example, parents with substance abuse or mental health issues should be assessed and offered treatment and support services to address the needs of the family as a whole. Supportive relationships with someone in a reentry case management role are key for youth to stabilize in the community.

Reentry is intrinsically a community-level concern and can provide support for ongoing rehabilitation and access to resources for employment, housing, and educational opportunities. Communities lack education about offender needs and risks. The reentry process could be improved through coordination with community leaders, community-based social services agencies and other community residents and volunteers that can provide cultural support, such as spiritual advisors, counselors and healers.

Although victim safety is considered highly important, victims are often uninformed about the status and whereabouts of offenders. If an offender has been incarcerated, he has probably not had the opportunity to make reparation and mend relationships prior to release. Inclusion of victim concerns is critical in reentry plans because those concerns could affect whether ex- offenders are accepted back into their families and communities. Strategies such as peacemaker courts can help to address the rehabilitation process.

III. Challenges in Long-Term (Prison) Reentry

Some Indian country jails have adults or juveniles serving sentences or commitments longer than a year, but most AI/AN offenders returning from long-term corrections have served time in off- reservation Federal Bureau of Prisons (BOP) or BIA facilities, or state prisons. In particular, AI/AN people living in P.L. 280 jurisdictions are most likely to serve time in state prisons located off-reservation because the state has criminal jurisdiction over crimes committed in Indian country.

The challenges tribes encounter with reentry from prisons differ from those involving jail reentry. A major difference is that tribes have minimal influence in how adult prisons and juvenile correctional systems are managed and operated by federal and state agencies. Consequently, tribes must have effective intergovernmental relationships to influence how AI/AN offenders are treated during their incarceration and the preparation they receive to return home. Some significant missing elements in reentry from prisons are regular coordination and information sharing with tribal justice staff, such as probation and parole officers to assist with reentry planning. Intergovernmental agreements may be necessary for federal and state agencies to proactively involve tribal justice agencies or other allied tribal agencies in reentry planning.

Intergovernmental relations may help alleviate resistance or reluctance by federal and state agencies in working with tribes through cross-agency training and education. Building knowledge, skills, and abilities across agencies should include cultural education, understanding state and federal correctional systems, working with Tribal Nations, developing collaborative reentry processes from federal and state correctional facilities to tribal communities, and understanding overlapping laws and policies. Agreements and contracts with off-reservation jails should include provision of programs and services, including enhancing skills of staff and programming on culturally appropriate elements.

System Challenges

Under the Major Crimes Act, the federal government may have concurrent jurisdiction over more serious crimes even if the crime occurred in Indian country. In these cases, the tribal or BIA facility may detain defendants after arrest and before they are turned over to the U.S. Marshals Service (USMS). If convicted and sentenced to confinement, an offender will then serve time in a BOP facility or contracted bed and the U.S.Probation and Pretrial Services will provide post-release supervision. As a result, reentry planning should include gathering data about tribal affiliation and building strategic partnerships with tribal and federal justice partners. Agreements should be drafted which set expectations for agency staff for collaboration, including roles and responsibilities, and education for agency staff on tribal jurisdiction and the cultural history, values and resources of those tribes. They should also share information about pre- and post-release risk assessments and services to assist in supporting a successful reentry.

Similar challenges face AI/AN persons convicted of offenses committed outside of Indian country, or if the state has jurisdiction to prosecute a crime committed in Indian country, especially with P.L. 280 states. In these cases, the state correctional staff may not be aware of offenders' AI/AN heritage or have the resources and staff time to develop strategies, given the long distance of federal and state prisons from many tribes and the logistical challenges to engaging family and community in transition planning.

Finally, federal agencies are responsible for ensuring tribal involvement with youth in federal custody who are placed in state or contracted juvenile facilities as there are no Federal Bureau of Prison (BOP) juvenile detention facilities. Tribal agencies may not be clear about where federal authority ends and state authority begins over youth reentry planning. Tribal liaisons in federal agencies are not the norm because of the lack of resources, staff, and time.

Tribal justice agencies such as adult and juvenile probation and parole officers can assist with reentry planning and facilitate coordination, information sharing, and case management. They are also critical partners in developing strategies to enhance the limited transitional services and tribal-based halfway houses on the reservation that are critical to the transition from long-term confinement. Many allied agencies are needed to provide the essential bundled services and resources to support returning ex-offenders and their families. Intergovernmental relationships are especially important for tribes located in P.L. 280 jurisdictions because in those states most tribal offenders serve adult sentences or juvenile commitments in state facilities.

Data, Infrastructure, and Program Challenges

Successful reentry of adults and juveniles requires enhanced services during and after incarceration. Acclimating to free society takes time and ex-offenders require training to cope with life after prison. They are held back by the lack of transitional living resources on or near tribal communities. An ex-offender may be placed in a halfway house or be supervised in a parole office that is far from the reservation. The ex-offender's support services such as treatment, employment, and education also may be located off the reservation, and transportation can be a problem.

Due to the lack of collaboration and information sharing discussed above, tribal justice systems may not be aware of an ex-offender's risks, needs, and history of interventions. This makes development of transition plans and community-based resources difficult both on the individual level and on the tribal level. Tribal Nations should be informed about who is coming into their communities, but even where the needs of the ex-offender are known, many Tribes face limited resources to support offender reentry, including treatment, housing, employment, and education. These communities need tools to help them assess and plan strategies to coordinate education, employment, and social, behavioral and mental health services. Some returning youth or adults, such as sex offenders, the learning disabled, or the elderly, may require extensive and specialized services, monitoring or supervision, and would benefit from a coordinated approach that leveraged the expertise of the BOP, FPS and state and local partners.

Challenges in Engaging Community and Family

Offenders returning from prison have been disconnected from their families, friends, and communities for a long time and may require support to rebuild trusting relationships with families and relatives or gain community acceptance. In some instances, reentry may have to focus on repairing damaged relationships with family members, relatives, and (as appropriate) victims and their families. Tribal members who serve longer sentences may also have to overcome stigma associated with their crimes.

Offenders may not know how, or may be reluctant, to contact their tribes or families after long- term confinement. The ex-offender may be confronted with negative family or peer influences and limited formal supports from the community. This can cause an adult offender to be released in urban areas where culturally relevant services and family support are difficult to obtain. Strategies to keep ex-offenders engaged in programs and services once they return home are essential to ensure ongoing attention to risks that could cause reoffending or relapse. The need for these strategies by AI/AN population enclaves outside of Indian country, such as nearby urban centers, should be considered. Coordination of these strategies may be most effective through collaboration with providers that specifically serve these unique and sometimes very large groups that maintain strong ties to their traditional homelands.

Tribes should be engaged in developing strategies to address the critical issues of community safety and housing options, especially for sex offenders or those convicted of drug-related crimes. Businesses can also be engaged to hire ex-offenders and to provide resources that will help them to write a resume, complete an application, practice interview techniques, establish good work habits and participate in mock job fairs. Finally, Tribal Leaders should be involved in reentry planning. They need to be notified by federal and state facilities through the tribe about offenders returning to their communities.

Tribes are diverse in their location, size and needs. They need reentry assistance that encompasses their values and history and includes planning for sustainability and continuity. Tribal Leaders discussed the need to engage families and communities in developing tribal justice strategies to reflect the values of tribes in developing holistic approaches to tribal justice.

A critical new resource for Tribal Nations in the area of reentry is the Second Chance Act (SCA). Under the SCA, funding and training and technical assistance are available to address a range of reentry needs including pre-release assessments and programming, community supervision and support, treatment for families of offenders including mothers and children, treatment for co-occurring disorders, mentoring of returning tribal members and employment in technology careers.

IV. Reentry Strategies Being Used In Indian Country

Below are a few examples of programs discussed in focus groups and consultations that suggest promising results.

- **Day School:** The Rosebud Sioux Tribe (Rosebud Sioux) and Todd County, S.D. created a day school in the JDC for detained and ex-offenders. Transportation is provided to ex- offenders to continue their education, and mental health services via video conference consultations allow for extended family participation.
- **Traditional Practices:** The Rosebud Sioux, Hualapai, and Mississippi Band of Choctaw Tribes provide traditional practices and healing ceremonies such as Sweat Lodge, Pipe Ceremony, and one-on-one sessions with an elder and a detained juvenile to address behavioral health issues. The San Carlos Apache Tribe in Arizona utilizes a traditional form of counseling for youth; bead therapy using

a talking circle format; use of elders to provide gender specific sweat lodges; and youth and family engagement.

- **Youth Green Reentry Program:** Hualapai JDC is in phase one of developing a "green building" class for detained youth, where they will develop skills and abilities to read and create "green blueprints" for sustainable green buildings in the community.
- **Family Group Decision Making Conferencing:** This restorative practices process, based in research, includes case management (pre- and post-release), strengthening families, achieving youth and family safety, and placing family at the center of the decision making process. The roots of FGDMC are from the Maori People in New Zealand.
- **Adult Community Support:** The Muscogee (Creek) Nation Reintegration Program in Oklahoma provides service to ex-offenders transitioning from a correctional facility back into the tribe. Services include parole and court advocacy; specialized reentry classes; clothing, food, and employment referrals; job advocacy; mental health and substance abuse referrals; educational opportunities; and temporary and long-term affordable housing.
- **Transitional Housing:** The Keweenaw Bay Indian Community Supportive Housing Program in Michigan provides safe and affordable housing and employment for tribal members and other Indians, recognizing the unique needs of individuals who are transitioning out of criminal justice facilities and treatment centers or who are coping with homelessness.
- **Federal Probation:** The Offender Orientation Program Serving Native American Offenders, developed by the District of New Mexico's Federal Probation and Parole Services, explains the roles of probation officers in the supervision process to enable the family members to understand that the ultimate goal is the offender's success. Post release, offenders and their families are required to attend an orientation meeting with federal probation and parole services, where supervision conditions and treatment requirements are reviewed.
- **Parent Strategies:** The Storybook Project by the Salt River Pima Maricopa Jail can help incarcerated parents provide positive interaction and modeling for their children during incarceration. The incarcerated parent is recorded reading a book, and the recording and book are sent to the child to listen and read along. In addition, under

SCA, funding can support family based treatment programs for both the incarcerated tribal member and their family.

V. Recommendations and Strategies

Elements of a Tribal Reentry Program

- **Jail reentry needs assessments, data collection and planning:** An important first step is for tribes to assess their reentry programming and services needs for adults and youth through data collection and analysis of information, including surveys and talking circles, program reviews, assessments of resources on or near Tribal Nations and gaps. Planning sessions with federal, tribal, state, and local practitioners to design and implement tribal reentry plans that evaluate needs, target populations, program effectiveness, and resources should be conducted. These plans should inform reentry policies and protocols for offenders being released into Tribal Nations from tribal and other authorities, including federal, state and local.
- **Critical elements of evidence-based reentry program:** All reentry programs should have some basic, evidence-based elements:
    - use of a risk assessment tool;
    - creation and management of an individual reentry plan;
    - access to AI/AN data collected by the tribe or the external agencies;
    - services to address identified needs, including education, mental health treatment, substance abuse treatment, impact of victimization or exposure to violence, life skills, job training, and mentoring;
    - structured reentry and reintegration from long-term confinement, and continuity of care at the community level; and
    - for those in jail short term, focus on alternatives to incarceration.
- **Elements in a tribal or BIA correctional facility:** BIA and tribally operated correctional facilities with other partners such as BIE and IHS have important roles in supporting efforts to coordinate the access of partners, provide pre-release programming that builds pro-social skills and reduces criminogenic needs to reduce recidivism. While a short jail term may limit the intensity of services, reentry plans should include local community based resources.

- **Elements in a contracted state prison or jail:** Within state facilities that are contractually or jurisdictionally housing AI/AN offender populations, pre- and post release services should be the same: risk assessments, reentry plans, and services including education, mental health treatment, substance abuse treatment, life skills, job training, and mentoring, and sharing information about pre-release assessments and programming.
- **Elements in a federal prison:** Most federal prisons offer critical support services pre- and post-release, including facility-based services in BOP facilities, specialized programming, transitional housing, and services and supervision. To be most effective, federal agencies such as BOP, FPS, and the Executive Office for U.S. Attorneys, National Indian Country Coordinator (USAO) should coordinate with BIA and tribal justice agencies on reentry planning and transition and information sharing about returning tribal members.
- **Transitional and halfway houses on tribal land:** Explore replication of promising practices such as the planning and construction of transitional living units in Indian country to address the demands and needs for adult and juvenile detention alternatives. Transitional living units allow for long-term residential settings for rehabilitation in a group living environment, and could be joined with other efforts in a Tribal Justice Center.
- **Supportive policy for federally incarcerated juveniles:** Explore the results of the recent Urban Institute report on juveniles under federal jurisdiction and explore impacts and recommended policy change for violent youth in federal custody. The plan should explore the roles of tribal and state juvenile justice and detention in supporting and housing these youth, as well as coordinate with tribal nations.
- **Tribal youth and adult engagement:** With support from DOJ's Tribal Youth Program and National Reentry Resource Center, develop a permanent forum for formerly detained AI/AN youth and adults to be at the table with federal, tribal, and state partners and be included in developing strategies to address the reentry issues they face and identify best practices that would yield better reentry results.

Short term resources that federal agencies will make available (within six months):

- DOJ's Second Chance Act's (SCA) Demonstration, Mentoring, Correctional Technology Jobs, Family Treatment and Co-Occurring Substance Abuse and Mental Health Disorders grant programs will support reentry activities, along with support from DOJ's National Reentry Resource Center.
- DOJ's Tribal Juvenile Detention and Reentry Green Demonstration Program funds vocational training programs to assist with job readiness (pre- and post-release). DOJ's Tribal Youth National Training and Technical Assistance and Tribal Juvenile Detention and Reentry Program Training and Technical Assistance can also assist.

Mid-term resources that federal agencies will make available (within twelve months):

- With DOI, DOJ and HHS, educate tribes on resources to support planning and funding such as SCA, Indian Alcohol and Substance Abuse Program (IASAP), Tribal Youth Program, IHS, Circles of Care, and the Tribal Action Plans.
- Provide forums for multidisciplinary teams to receive cross-agency training on issues related to the Tribal Justice Plan.
- Obtain results of the DOJ-funded LSI-R[60] validation project[61] in reference to AI/AN populations to inform development of assessment tool(s).
- Explore educational programming resources provided by DOI to address offender educational needs and incorporate the achievement of educational needs in reentry plans.
- Coordinate with the FPS and Pretrial Services Indian Country Steering Committee[62], to promote and encourage U.S. Probation/Pretrial Offices (USPO) to provide training in TLOA, coordinate with Steering Committee safety academies, share legal, evidence based practices and other related materials; support the partnership of the BOP and DOI with the tribes in arranging for halfway houses and other BOP contracts; and collaborate and partner across federal, state, tribal jurisdictions to ensure the optimal services delivery in relation to re-entry in Indian country.

- Coordinate with the USAO National Indian Country Coordinator, who will in turn coordinate with the Tribal Liaisons and Victim-Witness Specialists in USAOs having Indian country jurisdiction.
- The BOP and the Workgroup would assess the capacity and interest of tribes to undertake a halfway house program for tribal members who are returning from federal incarceration. Explore possible strategies to assist tribes in building the skills and infrastructure needed to support these activities for interested tribes.

Over the long term, if additional resources become available, it is also recommended that:

- DOJ, DOI, and the Workgroup assess and explore ways to build and enhance existing training, especially in juvenile justice and with state and local staff.
- The Workgroup review existing screening and assessment tools and develop culturally relevant tools that work for AI/AN populations in developing reentry plans.
- The Workgroup explore options to fund the construction of new transitional living or halfway houses or renovation of existing facilities to assist offenders returning to Tribal Nations.
- Support the collection of data and conducting more research on effective tribally driven reentry programming and the impact on recidivism of tribal members.
- DOJ and DOI would support transitional living facilities on tribal land by placing halfway houses within Multipurpose Justice Centers, but funding would be needed for planning, construction and operations.
- DOJ, in partnership with the Workgroup and in coordination with tribal partners, will lead strategies to build peer-to-peer learning and networking opportunities, including mentoring.
- Encourage federal, tribal, and state policy changes that promote the accessibility of tribal elders as resources, and to provide tribal best practices and traditional healing venues to detained and reentering tribal youth.

End Notes

[1] Steven W. Perry, *American Indians and Crime, A BJS Statistical Profile, 1992-2002*, U.S. Department of Justice, Bureau of Justice Statistics (2004), *available at* http://bjs.ojp.usdoj.gov/index.cfm?ty=pbdetail&iid=386.

[2] Six of the consultations were held by DOI and two were in coordination with the Tribal Justice, Safety and Wellness Sessions, which are Intergovernmental Consultations held by DOJ and DOI with Health and Human Services, Housing and Community Development, Small Business Association and the Corporation for National Community Service.

[3] Tribal Law and Policy Institute, 2010, "Obama Signs Tribal Law and Order Act," Tribal Law Updates, retrieved June 27, 2011 from tlpi.wordpress.com/2010/07/30/obama-signs-tribal-law-and-order-act/.

[4] The crimes include murder, manslaughter, kidnapping, maiming, felony sexual assault, incest, assault with intent to commit murder, assault with a dangerous weapon, assault resulting in serious bodily injury, assault against an individual who has not attained the age of 16 years, felony child abuse or neglect, arson, burglary, robbery, and felony theft.

[5] In both P.L. 280 and non-P.L. 280 jurisdictions, tribes retain concurrent jurisdiction over all crimes committed by Indians.

[6] This section of TLOA modifies sections of the Indian Law Enforcement Reform Act.

[7] The terms "Indian," "American Indian," "Alaska Native," and "Native American" refer to a person descended from ancestors indigenous to the lands that now constitute the United States. The term "Alaska Native" is by definition exclusive to peoples indigenous to Alaska. But as is the case for tribes located in the lower 48 states, the tribes in Alaska are culturally diverse, with unique circumstances, and rich traditions rooted in their regional homelands. Generally, the term "Native American" includes both American Indians of the lower 48 states and Alaska Natives. This document uses these terms interchangeably and may use the abbreviation of AI/AN.

[8] In October 2010, DOI hosted a series of six regional tribal consultations in San Diego, CA (October 12); Billings, MT (October 14); Albuquerque, NM (October 20); Prior Lake, MN (October 12) Oklahoma City, OK (October 26); and Miami, FL (October 28) to seek input about TLOA generally, including the Tribal Justice Plan. On December 8-9, 2010, DOJ hosted another consultation with Tribal Leaders in Palm Springs, CA, covering new tools authorized under TLOA and feedback on the Tribal Justice Plan. This last consultation was held in coordination with the Tribal Justice, Safety and Wellness Sessions, which are Intergovernmental Consultations held by DOJ and DOI with the Department of Health and Human Services, the Department of Housing and Community Development, the Small Business Administration and the Corporation for National and Community Service.

[9] The May 2011 consultation was also held in coordination with the Tribal Justice, Safety and Wellness Sessions described in footnote 10 above.

[10] The Focus Groups were in Rapid City, SD (April 19-20); Scottsdale, AZ (May 10 & 12); and Billings, MT (May 16-17).

[11] *Recidivism* refers to the concept of criminal recidivism, which is the process of reoffending or engaging in repeated criminal behavior. It can be measured as self-reported offenses, arrests and/or convictions. National Institute of Justice, *Do Drug Courts Work? Findings From Drug Court Research*, retrieved on June 25, 2011 from www.nij.gov/nij/topics/courts/drug-courts/work.htm.

[12] Pro-social skills help adolescents get along with others and navigate difficult social situations in positive ways. Pro-social skills include: social interaction skills; self control/anger management skills; and problem solving/conflict resolution skills. http://www.ncjjservehttp.org/NCJJWebsite/pdf/resourceguide/pro-social_Section 1.pdf.

[13] National Institute of Corrections, *Project Guide: Alternatives to Incarceration* (Washington, DC: Bureau of Prisons, National Institute of Corrections and the Native American and Alaskan Technical Assistance Project, 2005), 8.

[14] Ibid, 8-14

[15] Crime and Justice Institute, *Implementing Evidence-Based Practice in Community Corrections: The Principles of Effective Intervention* (Boston, MA: Crime and Justice Institute and U.S. Department of Justice, 2004).

[16] Ibid.

[17] Ibid.

[18] Feedback from TLOA Focus Group in Billings, MT on May 16-17, 2011.

[19] Because the majority of supervision cases are probation cases, the term "probation officer" will be used in lieu of "probation/parole officer."

[20] Kimberly A. Cobb, *A Desktop Guide for Tribal Probation Personnel: The Screening and Assessment Process* (Washington, DC: American Probation and Parole Association and U.S. Department of Justice, Bureau of Justice Assistance, 2011).

[21] If communities are considering developing a probation department, Fox Valley Technical College offers a DOJ funded Tribal Probation Academy, a 4-week course with an emphasis on topic areas specific to tribes that are not offered in other programs. Information about Fox Valley Technical College's Tribal Probation Academy can be found at www.fvtc.edu/public/content.aspx?ID=1240&PID=3.

[22] Tribal Law and Policy Institute, *Healing to Wellness Courts: A Preliminary Overview of Tribal Drug Courts* (West Hollywood, CA: Tribal Law and Policy Institute and U.S. Department of Justice, Office of Justice Programs, 1999). The National Institute of Justice (NIJ) has compiled feedback and evaluation data from the implementation of the first four Tribal Wellness Courts: Hualapai in Peach Springs, Arizona; Blackfeet in Browning, Montana; Fort Peck Reservation in Poplar, Montana; and Poarch Creek in Atmore, Alabama. Karen Gottlieb, *Lessons Learned in Implementing the First Four Tribal Wellness Courts* (Washington, DC: U.S. Department of Justice, Office of Justice Programs, National Institute of Justice, NCJ 231168, 2005).

[23] Program details can be found at: www.samhsa.gov/samhsanewsletter/Volume_18_Number_6/CirclesOfCare.aspx

[24] Stewart Wakeling and Miriam Jorgensen, *Strengthening and Rebuilding Tribal Justice Systems: A Participatory Outcomes Evaluation of the U.S. Department of Justice Comprehensive Indian Resources for Community and Law Enforcement (CIRCLE) Project* (Washington, DC: U.S. Department of Justice, Office of Justice Programs, National Institute of Justice, 2008).

[25] Peacemaker Courts are often associated with the Navajo but other tribal jurisdictions also use Peacemaker Courts. This discussion focuses on the Navajo Court because much has been written and published about that court.

[26] Raymond D. Austin, *Navajo Courts and Navajo Common Law: A Tradition of Tribal Self-Governance*, (Minneapolis, MN: University of Minnesota Press, 2009), 201.

[27] Ibid, 201. The Navajo Nation has expanded this pilot and currently has 242 certified Peacemakers and a Peacemaker Liaison in each of its 10 district courts who match disputants to appropriate Peacemakers.

[28] Anchorage Youth Court, retrieved on June 28, 2011 from www.anchorageyouthcourt.org/anchorageyouthcourt_about.html.

[29] Ibid.

[30] *Neither Safe Nor Secure: An Assessment of Indian Detention Facilities* (Washington, D.C.: US Department of the Interior, Office of Inspector General, No. 2004-I-0056, 2004), 31.

[31] BIA Detention Facilities Report, 2010, No. WR-EV-BIA-0005-2010. Can be accessed at http://www.doioig.gov/images/stories/reports/pdf/01%20WR-EV-BIA-0005-2010Public.pdf

[32] *Neither Safe Nor Secure,* 26.

[33] The Law Enforcement Assistance Administration (LEAA) was created by the 1968 Safe Streets Act and is the predecessor of the U.S. Department of Justice, Office of Justice Programs (OJP), Bureau of Justice Assistance (BJA).

[34] Initially, the CSCATL was authorized by Section 20109 of the Violent Crime Control and Law Enforcement Act of 1994, Pub. L. No. 104-134, codified at 42 U.S.C. § 13709(b), as legislation: amended, 42 U.S.C. Section 13709(b) and administered by the DOJ Corrections Program Office. It was a part of the Violent Offender Incarceration and Truth in Sentencing Incentive Grants program. Grants were issued for tribal projects in FY 1999. The Corrections Program Office, and its programs, was merged into the DOJ Bureau of Justice Assistance in 2003.

[35] This was formerly the Correctional Facilities on Tribal Lands program.

[36] In the very limited circumstances in which juveniles under the jurisdiction of the juvenile court can be detained in adult facilities, the separation core requirement of the Juvenile Justice and Delinquency Prevention Act of 1974 requires that states provide that juveniles being detained must be separated by "sight and sound" from adult inmates. Compliance by tribal facilities is strongly encouraged.

[37] Indian tribes and tribal organizations may enter into agreements with the federal government to manage DOI and/or IHS programs that impact their members, resources and governments pursuant to agreements with the federal government in accordance with the Indian Self-Determination and Education Assistance Act of 1975 (P.L. 93-638) and the 1994 amendments to that law. These agreements are commonly referred to as either "638 contracts" or "self-governance compacts" and have very similar goals and objectives.

[38] The PONI training was developed by CPO and the National Institute of Corrections as the training and technical assistance partner.

[39] Such as the FBI, Bureau of Prisons (BOP), Border Patrol (CBP), and the DEA.

[40] *2009 Means Index of Construction (*National Institute of Corrections, Planning of New Institutions Program).

[41] ***Personnel services worksheet:*** Staffing costs generally account for 70 to 80 percent of the jail budget. Because this is such a large portion of the budget request, estimating personnel expenses is a key step in budget development. A staffing plan is essential for establishing a budget plan that will provide for the personnel resources needed to run the jail. The staffing plan details the number and type of personnel needed to provide adequate 24 hour coverage and to conduct all essential jail functions. This information is used to complete a personal services worksheet. NIC, *Budget Guide for Jail Administrators,* Developing the Budget, 17.

[42] T.R. Clear, G.F. Cole & M.D. Reisig, M. D., American Corrections (Belmont, CA: Thomas Wadsworth, 2006).

[43] Todd Minton, *Jails in Indian Country, 2009,* (Washington, DC: U.S. Department of Justice, Bureau of Justice Statistics, 2011), 9.

[44] For example, a correctional officer is paid about $75,000 annually while support positions would be paid about $50,000 annually.

[45] James K. Whittaker, "The Reinvention of Residential Treatment: An Agenda for Research and Practice," *Child and Adolescent Psychiatric Clinics of North America* (2004),13:267–78. These figures reflect placements of all children, not just American Indian children.

[46] Andrea J. Sedlak, and Karla S. McPherson, *Conditions of Confinement: Findings From the Survey of Youth in Residential Placement (*Washington, D.C.: U.S. Department of Justice, Office of Justice Programs, 2010).

[47] Trauma Exposure in American Indian/ Alaska Native Children (Big Foot: Willmon-Haque & Braden, 2008) 3.

[48] Tribal Youth in the Federal Justice System. Draft Final Report. Urban Institute Justice Policy Center, February, 2011. *As document is forthcoming, no page number is available.*

[49] *2009 Means Index of Construction Costs (*National Institute of Corrections, Planning of New Institutions Program).

[50] Some Indian communities are located in geographic areas that have expansive soils and similar site characteristics that make construction of large facilities difficult. Significant parts of reservations have expansive soils, particularly in North Dakota, South Dakota, New Mexico and Arizona. It is often difficult to calculate soil quality, and this can have a significant, negative impact on project budgets.

[51] www.reentry.gov

[52] A.P Melton,"Indigenous Justice Systems and Tribal Society," *Judicature* (1995),79(3) 126–133; L. Bond- Maupin, C. Chicago Lujan, and M. Bortner, "Jailing of American Indian Adolescents," *Crime, Law and Social Change*(1995) 23:1–16; C. Zuni, "Strengthening What Remains," *Kansas Journal of Law and Public Policy* (1997), 7(18); J.Zion, "The Dynamics of Navajo Peacemaking," *Journal of Contemporary Criminal Justice* (1998)14(1):58–74; B.J. Jones, *Role of Indian Tribal Courts in the Justice System*, Native American Topic-Specific Monograph Series, March 2000.

[53] TLOA Focus Group, Billings, MT, May 16-17, 2011.

[54] Todd Minton, *Jails in Indian Country, 2009, (*Washington, DC: U.S. Department of Justice, Bureau of Justice Statistics, 2011), 2.

[55] William Adams and Julie Samuels, *Tribal Youth in the Federal Justice System,*(Washington DC: Urban Institute Report, 2011), 25.

[56] The number of jails noted here is intended to provide context for the data provided by these tribal jails in the BJS survey. In addition to these 80 tribes, other tribes contract with state or local facilities to house those tribal members detained or incarcerated through their tribal justice centers.

[57] Minton, *Jails in Indian Country,* 8.

[58] Criminogenic factors are 1) anti-social personality, 2) anti-social attitudes and values, 3) anti-social associates, 4) family dysfunction, 5) poor self-control, 6) poor problem-solving skills, 7) substance abuse, and 8) lack of employment and/or employment skills.

[59] There are some strong examples of collaboration to support these goals. See Walking on Common Ground at http://walkingoncommonground.org/; and the New York Federal, State Tribal Courts Forum at http://www.nyfedstatetribalcourtsforum.org/history.shtml

[60] Level of Service Inventory-Revised.

[61] This project is being led by the Crime and Justice Institute.

[62] The Indian Country Steering Committee (ICSC) is a partnership between the chiefs of several districts with high AI/AN populations, and the Office of Probation and Pretrial Services to identify issues, trends, needs, and best practices.

In: Tribal Law and Order
Editor: Judy Conlon
ISBN: 978-1-63117-152-9

Chapter 2

TRIBAL LAW AND ORDER ACT: NONE OF THE SURVEYED TRIBES REPORTED EXERCISING THE NEW SENTENCING AUTHORITY, AND THE DEPARTMENT OF JUSTICE COULD CLARIFY TRIBAL ELIGIBILITY FOR CERTAIN GRANT FUNDS*

United States Government Accountability Office

Congressional Requesters

The Tribal Law and Order Act of 2010 (TLOA) recognizes that instances of crime have increased on Indian reservations, and concerns have been raised as to whether tribal courts are able to impose sentences stringent enough to help deter such criminal activity.[1] Prior to the enactment of TLOA, federal law limited tribal courts to imposing prison terms of no greater than 1-year per offense for convicted defendants. We reported in February 2011 that tribal officials said that the 1-year limit on prison sentences did not serve as an effective deterrent against criminal activity and may have contributed to the high levels of crime and repeat offenders in Indian country.[2] We also reported that, as a result of the limited sentencing authorities of tribal courts, tribes will

* This is an edited, reformatted and augmented version of the United States Government Accountability Office publication, GAO-12-658R, dated May 30, 2012.

often rely on the federal government to investigate and prosecute more serious offenses, such as homicide, because a successful federal prosecution of such offenders could result in a lengthier prison sentence and better ensure justice for victims of crime in Indian country. However, acknowledging that tribal justice systems are often the most appropriate institutions for maintaining law and order in Indian country, TLOA states that its purpose is to, among other things, empower tribal governments to effectively provide public safety and reduce the prevalence of violent crime in Indian country. For example, TLOA authorizes tribal courts to impose upon certain convicted defendants terms of imprisonment of up to 3 years per offense, provided the tribes afford certain rights to defendants, which are discussed below.

We reported in May 2012 on the extent to which the Department of Justice (DOJ) and the Bureau of Indian Affairs (BIA) within the Department of the Interior (DOI) provide federal funding and other assistance that may be used to support indigent defense, including in Indian country.[3]

Federal law does not entitle an indigent Indian defendant prosecuted in a tribal court to a licensed defense attorney provided at the tribal government's expense unless a sentence in excess of 1-year per offense as authorized under TLOA is sought. Therefore, as part of our indigent defense review and in response to your request, we asked tribes about their plans to implement this as well as the other requirements necessary to exercise TLOA's new sentencing authority. Specifically, this report addresses the following questions:

(1) To what extent did selected tribes report that they exercise, or have plans to exercise, TLOA's new sentencing authority, and that they implement, or have plans to implement its associated requirements, and what challenges, if any, did the selected tribes report in doing so?
(2) What types of assistance did federal agencies report that they provide to assist tribes in exercising TLOA's new sentencing authority, and what, if any, federal assistance did selected tribes report that they would like to receive?

To answer both objectives, we surveyed all 171 tribes (out of the 566 federally-recognized tribes as of January 3, 2012) that (1) reported allocating Tribal Priority Allocations (TPA)—federal funding that BIA distributes to tribes and that tribes may allocate to a variety of activities—to their tribal courts (referred to as the "Tribal Courts TPA") (142 out of 171), (2) were awarded the Edward Byrne Memorial Justice Assistance Grant (JAG) by DOJ (2 out of 171), or (3) both allocated funding to their Tribal Courts TPA and received JAG funding (27 out of 171) in any fiscal year from 2005 through 2010.[4] We selected these tribes because they allocated federal funding to their Tribal Courts TPA, and therefore operated tribal courts during this time period. In addition, we selected these same tribes for surveys we conducted from December 2011 through February 2012 for the purposes of our review of the extent to which federal funding is used to support state, local, and tribal indigent defense services.[5] In developing the two questionnaires sent to Tribal Courts TPA and JAG recipients, we consulted with 2 tribal associations and pre- tested the questionnaires with 4 tribes. In our surveys, we asked the tribes about their plans to exercise the new sentencing authority TLOA provides. Generally, tribal court officials such as the chief judge, court administrator, or court clerk completed the questionnaire. We attempted to contact nonrespondents multiple times by email, phone, and fax during the survey to encourage them to complete and submit the questionnaire, and conducted abbreviated phone interviews on key questions with a subset of those tribes. Of the 171 tribes, 109 responded to the section of our surveys regarding TLOA's new sentencing authority, thus resulting in a 64 percent response rate. (See encl. I for our survey questions and results.) Because we surveyed only those tribes that allocated or received federal funding for their tribal courts, and not all of them responded, the results from this survey cannot be generalized to all tribes; however, the responses provided us with information on the perspectives of selected tribes' plans to exercise the new sentencing authority.[6] We also interviewed the following entities regarding the impact of the new sentencing authority on tribal public safety and justice programs: BIA officials responsible for activities related to tribal courts; DOJ officials responsible for advising the department on tribal matters, interacting with tribes, and administering tribal grant funding; tribal experts, such as officials from the National Congress of American Indians (NCAI), because it serves as the major national tribal government organization; and tribal court officials at 3 tribes we visited, at 2 additional tribes with which we pretested our survey, and at 9 other tribes because they reported allocating federal funding for indigent defense in our survey. In selecting the tribes we visited or with which we conducted pretests, we considered diversity across factors such as their location, the amount and type of federal funding they received, and whether the tribe employed a public defender to help ensure that we obtained a range of perspectives. The views of these tribes are not generalizable, but provide valuable insights into selected tribes' decisions to exercise the new sentencing authority.

We conducted this performance audit from February 2012 through May 2012 in accordance with generally accepted government auditing standards. Those standards require that we plan and perform the audit to obtain sufficient, appropriate evidence to provide a reasonable basis for our findings and conclusions based on our audit objectives. We believe that the evidence obtained provides a reasonable basis for our findings and conclusions based on our audit objectives.

RESULTS IN BRIEF

Among the tribes that responded to our survey (109), none reported that they were exercising TLOA's new sentencing authority, and, in open-ended responses, many tribes (86 of 90, or 96 percent) reported challenges to exercising this authority due to funding limitations. Tribes were relatively evenly split among those that reported that they have plans to exercise the new authority (36 of 101, or 36 percent); that they did not know the tribe's plans to exercise the new authority (34 of 101, or 34 percent) because, for instance, the tribal council has not yet made a decision; and that they did not have plans to do so (31 of 101, or 31 percent).[7] In addition, 64 percent of selected tribes (70 of 109) reported implementing at least half of the requirements necessary for exercising the new sentencing authority, but reported challenges in implementing other requirements. Specifically, these tribes most frequently reported implementing the requirement to maintain a record of the criminal proceeding, and least frequently reported providing the defendant a licensed defense attorney. For example, 8 tribes that described challenges to exercising the new sentencing authority reported challenges with the costs of implementing the requirements associated with the sentencing authority. In particular, 3 tribes reported challenges with the costs of providing a licensed judge with sufficient legal training as required under TLOA. As a result, tribal courts may be unable to impose prison sentences of over 1 year to 3 years per offense—as TLOA provides—and possibly provide a more effective deterrent to criminal activity in Indian country.

DOJ and BIA provide funding and technical assistance to tribes that can be used to help them exercise the new sentencing authority, and tribes reported that they desire additional funding and technical assistance from the federal government for this purpose. However, tribes do not always have a clear understanding about their eligibility for federal funding sources available to help them exercise the new sentencing authority. In its fiscal year 2011 solicitation for the Tribal Civil and Criminal Legal Assistance (TCCLA) grant, DOJ stated that consistent with its authorizing statute, eligibility is "limited to tribal and non-tribal non-profit (Internal Revenue Code (I.R.C.) § 501(c)(3)) entities that provide legal assistance services for federally recognized Indian tribes, members of federally recognized Indian tribes, or tribal justice systems pursuant to the federal poverty guidelines."[8] However, 6 of the 9 tribes or tribal entities that applied for TCCLA in fiscal year 2011 were ineligible—because they were not 501(c)(3) non-profit entities—yet DOJ did not explain to the tribes that they were ineligible for funding because they were not such entities. As a result, these tribes used resources to prepare applications explaining their intended use of the funding—which, for 4 of the 6 tribes, was to meet requirements necessary for exercising the new sentencing authority—when they were not eligible for the funding. DOJ officials agreed that they could update the letter used to inform applicants that they were not selected for funding to make it clearer that only 501(c)(3) nonprofit entities are eligible. Further, internal control standards state that agency management should ensure that there are adequate means of communicating with external stakeholders that may have a significant impact on the agency achieving its goals.[9] By taking actions to better clarify that applicants must be 501(c)(3) non-profit entities to be eligible for TCCLA, both during the application process and when applicants are notified of their ineligibility, DOJ could better ensure that the tribes and DOJ will not use resources to prepare, review, and deny applications for grants for which tribes or certain tribal entities are not eligible. Moreover, tribes would also be better positioned to make informed decisions about the available funds to pursue.

We are recommending that DOJ take actions—both during the application process and when applicants are notified of their ineligibility—to better clarify the circumstances under which applicants, including tribes or tribal entities, are eligible or ineligible for TCCLA funds. DOJ concurred with the recommendation.

BACKGROUND

Whether or not tribes have jurisdiction to investigate and prosecute crimes that occur in Indian country depends on various factors, including the nature of the crime, whether or not the alleged offender or victim is Indian, and whether jurisdiction has been conferred on a particular entity by, for example, federal treaty or statue.[10] As a general principle, the federal government recognizes

Indian tribes as "distinct, independent political communities" that "remain a separate people, with the power of regulating their internal and social relations," which includes enacting substantive law over internal matters and enforcing that law in their own forums.[11] The federal government, however, has authority to regulate or modify the power of self-government that tribes otherwise possess, and has exercised this authority to establish an intricate web of jurisdiction over crime in Indian country.[12] For example, tribal and federal jurisdiction is generally concurrent, meaning both the tribal governments and federal government, independent and exclusive of the other, may prosecute the alleged offender, where the alleged offender is Indian but the victim is non-Indian. Federal jurisdiction is generally exclusive where the alleged offender is non-Indian and the victim is Indian; and depending on the nature of the crime, tribal jurisdiction may be exclusive where the alleged offender and the victim are Indian.[13]

Tribes, which retain limited, inherent sovereignty, are not bound by restraints placed upon the federal or state governments through the Bill of Rights or other amendments to the U.S. Constitution.[14] When a tribal government exercises its jurisdiction to prosecute an Indian offender, however, it must do so in accordance with the Indian Civil Rights Act (ICRA). Enacted in 1968, ICRA limited the extent to which tribes may exercise their powers of self-government by imposing conditions on tribal governments similar to those found in the Bill of Rights to the U.S. Constitution.[15] For example, ICRA extends the protections of free speech, free exercise of religion, and due process and equal protection under tribal laws.[16] Tribes must also afford a defendant the rights to a speedy and public trial, to be informed of the nature and cause of the accusation, and to be represented by counsel at the defendant's own expense, among other things.[17] ICRA also governs the sentencing authority tribes may exercise over convicted Indian offenders. Prior to the enactment of TLOA, ICRA provided that tribes could only sentence a convicted defendant to a term of imprisonment not to exceed 1-year per offense. With the enactment of TLOA in July 2010, tribal courts are able to impose upon convicted defendants, in defined circumstances, terms of imprisonment not to exceed 3 years for any offense.[18]

To exercise the new sentencing authority, however, tribes must have met the following requirements:

- afford the defendant the right to effective assistance of counsel at least equal to that guaranteed by the United States Constitution;

- if the defendant is indigent, provide the defendant with a licensed defense attorney at the tribe's expense;[19]
- ensure that a judge licensed to practice law in any jurisdiction in the United States presides over the proceeding;
- ensure that the judge has sufficient legal training to preside over criminal proceedings;
- prior to charging the defendant, make publicly available the tribal government's criminal laws and rules of evidence and criminal procedure; and
- maintain a record of the criminal proceedings, including an audio or other recording of the trial proceedings.

In addition, TLOA established the Indian Law and Order Commission (Commission), which is responsible for conducting a comprehensive study of law enforcement and criminal justice in tribal communities.[20]

DOI and DOJ are the two primary federal agencies that provide support to federally-recognized tribes to, among other purposes, help them administer justice. Within DOI, BIA is responsible for supporting tribes in their efforts to ensure public safety and administer justice within their reservations as well as to provide related services directly or through contracts or compacts with federally-recognized tribes.[21] To that end, BIA's Office of Justice Services—which was established by TLOA—supports tribal law enforcement, detention, and court programs.[22] Within the Office of Justice Services, the Division of Tribal Justice Support for Courts works with tribes to establish and maintain tribal judicial systems. This includes conducting assessments of tribal courts and providing training and technical assistance on a range of topics, including establishing or updating law and order codes. Further, BIA distributes funding that tribes may allocate to their tribal courts through its Tribal Courts TPA. All federally–recognized tribes are eligible to receive TPA funds.[23] DOJ provides grant funding, training, and technical assistance to federally-recognized tribes to enhance the capacity of tribal courts, among other tribal justice programs, through its Office of Justice Programs. This includes JAG, a formula grant program that is a source of federal justice funding to state, local, and tribal governments. In addition, pursuant to TLOA, the Attorney General established the Office of Tribal Justice within DOJ to facilitate coordination for federally-recognized tribal governments and tribal organizations seeking assistance or information from DOJ on issues related to public safety and justice in Indian country.[24]

A THIRD OF SELECTED TRIBES PLAN TO EXERCISE TLOA'S SENTENCING AUTHORITY, BUT TRIBES MOST FREQUENTLY REPORTED THAT THEY DID NOT HAVE FUNDS TO DO SO

None of the 109 tribes that responded to our survey reported that they were currently exercising the new sentencing authority. Among these tribes, 36 of 101 (36 percent) reported that they have plans to exercise the new authority; 34 of 101 (34 percent) reported that they did not know the tribe's plans to exercise the new authority because, for instance, the tribal council has not yet made a decision; and 31 of 101 (31 percent) reported that they did not have plans to do so.[25] A tribal official who reported that his tribe has plans to exercise the new authority stated that the tribe decided to do so because the authority permitted the tribe the flexibility to sentence for 3 years if necessary. Specifically, the official stated that because the reservation is near a metropolitan area, the tribe encounters many cross-jurisdictional crimes—such as gang activity—and the authority to sentence up to 3 years would allow the tribe to more effectively control crime.

Although tribes did not report exercising the new sentencing authority, 64 percent of these tribes (70 of 109) reported that they currently implement at least half of the associated requirements for exercising the new sentencing authority. These tribes most frequently reported maintaining a record of the criminal proceeding and least frequently reported providing the defendant a licensed attorney. For example, officials from one tribe reported difficulty attracting licensed attorneys to work for the tribe who are knowledgeable about Indian law. Another tribe reported that its judges are not law-trained and that only males are allowed to serve as judges.[26] Figure 1 shows, for each requirement necessary to exercise the new sentencing authority, the number of tribes that reported they were currently implementing the requirement, have plans to implement it, or have no plans to do so.

Tribes that described challenges to exercising the new sentencing authority most frequently identified limited funding (86 of 90, or 96 percent). For instance, 8 of these 90 tribes identified challenges with the costs of implementing the requirements associated with the sentencing authority. In addition, 12 of the 90 (13 percent) tribes reported that the costs associated with longer sentences presented a challenge to exercising the new sentencing authority. For instance, 1 tribe stated that although the tribe implements all requirements necessary for exercising the new authority, it has chosen not to do so because it does not have the funding to support other activities that would result from implementing the new sentencing authority, such as probation. Moreover, 3 of the 90 tribes reported challenges with the costs of hiring a licensed, law-trained judge. For example, 1 tribe reported that it has maintained a very effective criminal and civil justice system for the past 40 years—which has never had or required a law- trained judge to preside over the court system—and that the costs associated with hiring a law- trained judge from outside of the community would be unreasonable. Furthermore, in our indigent defense review, 52 percent (24 of 46) of tribes that reported they did not provide indigent defense services in any year from fiscal years 2005 through 2010 also reported that they did not have sufficient funding to provide these services.[27]

In addition, 36 of 90 (40 percent) tribes identified limitations of their tribal codes and constitutions as a challenge to exercising the new sentencing authority, and 33 of 90 (37 percent) tribes reported that their tribal codes would need to be revised to take advantage of the new sentencing authority. For example, 1 tribe reported that the tribe's constitution sets forth minimal requirements for tribal court judges, which would not meet the requirement of a licensed, law-trained judge necessary to exercise the new sentencing authority. Another tribe reported that its tribal constitution currently limits the tribal court's sentencing authority to 1 year. One of these tribes estimated that it would take at least 1 year for its council to approve rewriting the tribal codes and another year to rewrite them.

In addition to tribes, officials from DOJ's Office of Tribal Justice, the Indian Law and Order Commission (Commission), NCAI, and BIA also identified factors that could help to explain why tribes do not have plans to exercise the new sentencing authority. For example, consistent with statements made by an official from the Office of Tribal Justice, some tribes may be planning to exercise the authority, but have not currently done so because they may be waiting to see whether tribes that have exercised the authority have been subject to litigation as a result or whether such sentences will withstand appeal. In addition, officials from NCAI and BIA reported that some tribes may view the new sentencing authority and the associated requirements as incompatible with traditional notions of tribal justice. For example, an official from NCAI stated that some tribes have a fundamental opposition to incarceration as a means of punishment and instead choose traditional means of justice that incorporate healing and rehabilitation, as opposed to detention. Moreover, a BIA official stated that the process for tribes to update tribal codes and constitutions to reflect provisions in TLOA will take time and money.

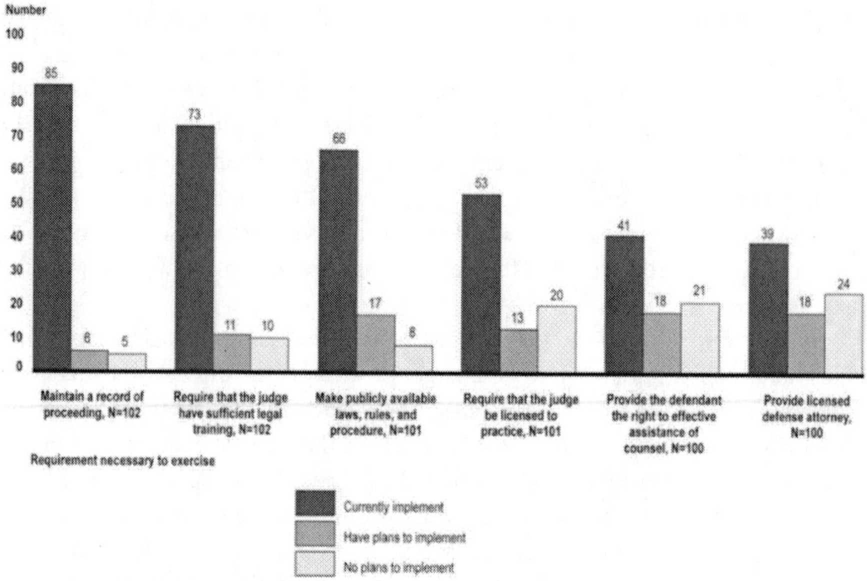

Source: GAO analysis of survey responses.

Note: Some tribes answered "don't know" or did not provide an answer, so each item does not total 109.

Figure 1. Number of Surveyed Tribes That Reported Implementing Requirements Necessary to Exercise TLOA's Sentencing Authority.

DOJ Could Clarify Eligibility for Funding It Provides to Tribes, and Tribes Reported That More Funding and Training Would Help Them Exercise TLOA's Sentencing Authority

BIA and DOJ Provide Funding and Technical Assistance to Tribes, but DOJ Could Clarify Tribes' Eligibility for Funding

Both BIA and DOJ provide funding that tribes could use to help meet the necessary requirements for exercising the new sentencing authority. According to BIA officials, tribal courts receive funding through BIA's annual Tribal Courts TPA distributions in the form of contracts or compacts.[28] Tribes select among available TPAs, such as tribal courts and social services, and then determine how much BIA funding to allocate to each of these TPAs. Further, tribes may generally reallocate funding from one TPA activity to another according to their needs. For example, a tribe needing more funds for tribal courts than for natural resources management may move funds to meet those needs. In fiscal year 2011, 141 tribes allocated $24.7 million of BIA contracts and compacts to their tribal courts for salaries and related administrative costs of judges, prosecutors, public defenders, court clerks, probation officers, juvenile officers, and other court support staff through the Tribal Courts TPA. In addition, DOJ officials identified the Coordinated Tribal Assistance Solicitation (CTAS) as a resource for tribes that reported needing additional funding to exercise the new sentencing authority. In fiscal year 2011, DOJ awarded, through CTAS, $82 million to tribal justice system and juvenile justice programs that could be used to exercise the new sentencing authority, such as maintaining a record of the criminal proceeding and hiring court-appointed defenders for juvenile offenders.[29]

In addition, DOJ and BIA provide training and other assistance to tribes, which could assist them in exercising the new sentencing authority. For instance, DOJ (through Access to Justice and the U.S. Attorneys' Offices), BIA, and the Administrative Office of the U.S. Courts' (AOUSC) Offices of Defender Services (through the federal public defender offices) have partnered to develop the Tribal Court Trial Advocacy Training Program, which consists of a series of trainings for tribal court personnel, including defenders, prosecutors, and judges.[30] According to a DOJ official involved in the training, this training could help tribes meet the requirement in TLOA that a judge presiding over the criminal proceeding have sufficient legal training. The first such training occurred in August 2011, and the second in March 2012. According to DOJ and BIA officials, an additional six trainings are planned through January 2013. In addition, BIA provides court recording devices to tribes, which could help tribes in implementing the requirement to maintain a record of criminal proceedings. According to BIA officials, as of May 2012, BIA provided over 60 recording devices for tribal courts and plans to provide an additional 15 to tribes that requested the device.

Moreover, a DOJ official stated that the Tribal Civil and Criminal Legal Assistance (TCCLA) grant could be used to support tribes' efforts to exercise the new sentencing authority. In particular, certain types of tribes (which we discuss below) could use funding in one of the grant categories—Category 2, which is available for criminal legal assistance—to hire a law-trained public defender. However, tribes were not always clear on whether they met eligibility requirements for the grant.[31] The statute establishing TCCLA states that eligibility is limited to nonprofit entities, as defined under section 501(c)(3) of the Internal Revenue Code. DOJ's fiscal year 2010 TCCLA solicitation did not specify that eligibility was limited to 501(c)(3) nonprofit entities, but DOJ adjusted its fiscal year 2011 TCCLA solicitation to include that eligibility for TCCLA is "limited to tribal and non-tribal non-profit (Internal Revenue Code (I.R.C.) § 501(c)(3)) entities that provide legal assistance services for Indian tribes, members of Indian tribes, or tribal justice systems pursuant to federal poverty guidelines."[32] DOJ grant program officials stated that they made this change because their Office of General Counsel indicated that the statute limited eligibility to 501(c)(3) nonprofit entities. However, this phrasing could be read as "tribal entities" and "non-tribal non-profit (Internal Revenue Code (I.R.C.) § 501(c)(3)) entities" are eligible for the funding, and as not restricting eligibility to "tribal non-profit (Internal Revenue Code (I.R.C.) § 501(c)(3)) entities." For instance, even after DOJ changed the solicitation language, an official from one tribe reported applying in fiscal year 2011 for TCCLA because, based on eligibility requirements, the individual understood that, as a division of tribal government, the individual's office qualified as a tribal entity when it was actually ineligible because it was not a 501(c)(3) entity. Of the nine tribal governments or tribal entities that applied for TCCLA in fiscal year 2011, six were uncertain about their eligibility and applied, despite not being 501(c)(3) nonprofits, and were denied by DOJ. As a result, six tribes expended resources to apply for TCCLA although they were ineligible, and four of these tribes planned to use the funding to exercise the new sentencing authority.

In addition to these tribes being uncertain about their eligibility when applying for TCCLA, certain tribes continued to be uncertain about their eligibility even after receiving a letter from DOJ explaining why they were not selected for funding. In particular, of the 3 tribes we interviewed regarding TCCLA all 3 reported that after they received this letter from DOJ, they still did not understand why they were ineligible. The letters sent to these tribes stated that the tribes were not eligible because they were not nonprofit entities. What the letters did not explain was that the tribes were ineligible because they are not 501(c)(3) nonprofit entities. DOJ officials agreed that the letter could be updated to clarify that only 501(c)(3) nonprofit entities are eligible. Internal control standards state that agency management should ensure that there are adequate means of communicating with external stakeholders that may have a significant impact on the agency achieving its goals.[33] By taking actions to better clarify TCCLA's eligibility requirements both during the application process and when applicants are notified of their ineligibility, DOJ could better ensure that neither the tribes nor DOJ will use resources to prepare, review, and deny applications for grants for which tribes are not eligible, and consequently enable tribes to make informed decisions about funding sources.

Tribes Reported That More Funding and Training Would Be Beneficial

While DOJ and BIA provide funding, training, and technical assistance, tribes that responded to our survey and identified assistance they would like to receive from the federal government (86 of 109) most frequently reported that more of this type of support from the federal government would help them exercise the new sentencing authority.

- For instance, tribes reported that they would like to build or expand a detention facility on the reservation (10); receive additional funding to employ a licensed attorney to provide indigent defense services (2); and hire a licensed, law-trained judge (2), among other things.
- In addition, 15 tribes reported that they would like technical assistance and guidance on the new sentencing authority and the necessary requirements. For example, 1 tribe identified assistance such as guidance from BIA and local U.S. Attorneys' Offices regarding how to implement the new sentencing authority.
- Eleven tribes also identified instances where the federal government could share information to help tribes exercise the new sentencing authority, such as by developing a fact sheet.

Both DOJ and BIA have taken actions to increase funding and training to tribes in this area. In its fiscal year 2012 CTAS solicitation, DOJ officials reported that they made a number of changes to reflect tribes' needs for additional resources with the passage of TLOA. For instance, DOJ added the implementation of enhanced authorities and provisions under TLOA as a goal under the justice systems, and alcohol and substance abuse purpose area. In addition, DOJ also announced a new program for fiscal year 2012, the Tribal Justice System Capacity Building Training and Technical Assistance program, which seeks to enhance tribal justice information sharing and meet tribal justice system capacity building needs, among other things.[34] Further, in its fiscal year 2013 budget justification, BIA recognized tribes' need for additional resources, and asked for $1 million in additional Tribal Courts TPA funding to help meet that need.[35] In particular, to support the new sentencing authority given to tribal courts in TLOA, BIA requested additional funding to be used for tribal court staff salaries, among other things. According to BIA, tribal court systems were struggling financially to operate under the pre-TLOA requirements, and implementation of TLOA requires additional resources. For example, according to BIA's budget justification, should a tribal court exercise the sentencing authority extended by TLOA, additional training on developing tribal sentencing guidelines will be required for tribal court judges and other personnel. BIA expects that the amount of funding requested would significantly improve the ability of the tribal courts to effectively implement TLOA, among other things. In addition, BIA has partnered with the National Judicial College to provide scholarships in 2012 and 2013 for two members of each of the 141 tribal courts that allocate to the Tribal Courts TPA to each attend two courses.[36] These courses could include Appellate Skills for Tribal Judges and Advanced Tribal Court Management. Moreover, according to BIA, it has established a new process for conducting tribal court reviews that will allow it to assess the unmet needs of tribal courts, including those related to the implementation of the requirements necessary to exercise TLOA's new sentencing authority, by the end of 2013.

CONCLUSION

The new sentencing authority under TLOA provides tribal courts with the opportunity to impose sentences of more than 1 year to 3 years per offense and possibly provide a more effective deterrent to criminal activity in Indian country. Tribes reported that funding and technical assistance from DOJ and BIA could assist them in exercising the new authority. However, some tribes expressed uncertainty regarding their eligibility for certain funds. Specifically, DOJ did not inform tribes that applied for TCCLA grants, which could be used to help meet the requirements necessary to exercise the new sentencing authority, that they were deemed ineligible because they were not 501(c)(3) nonprofit entities. By taking actions to better clarify that applicants must be 501(c)(3) nonprofit entities to be eligible for TCCLA, both during the application process and when applicants are notified of their ineligibility, DOJ could better ensure that the tribes and DOJ will not use resources to prepare, review, and deny applications for grants for which tribes or certain tribal entities are not eligible.

Recommendation for Executive Action

To help ensure that tribes better understand which grant resources could assist tribes in exercising the new sentencing authority, we recommend that the Assistant Attorney General of the Office of Justice Programs take actions—both during the application process and when applicants are notified of their ineligibility—to better clarify the circumstances under which applicants, including tribes and tribal entities, are eligible or ineligible for TCCLA funds.

Agency Comments and Our Evaluation

We provided a draft of this report for review and comment to DOJ and DOI. In addition, we provided relevant sections of the report to NCAI and the Commission. We received written comments from DOJ. In its written comments, DOJ concurred with the recommendation that it take actions to better clarify the circumstances under which applicants, including tribes and tribal entities, are eligible or ineligible for TCCLA funds, and identified several actions that the Office of Justice Programs has taken and will take to do so. These actions include updating the fiscal year 2012 TCCLA solicitation to clarify eligibility language, revising language in letters sent to fiscal year 2012 TCCLA applicants that were not selected for funding to explain why they were ineligible, and developing a web page to provide information on resources for legal assistance and indigent defense services and activities available for tribes. These actions, when implemented, should address the intent of our recommendation. In an email dated May 17, 2012, DOI's liaison stated that DOI does not have written comments to include in our report. DOJ, DOI, and the Commission also provided technical comments, which we incorporated throughout the report as appropriate.

Eileen R. Larence
Director, Homeland Security and Justice Issues

ENCLOSURE

Enclosure I: Survey Questions and Responses

To gather information on whether tribes are implementing the Tribal Law and Order Act's (TLOA) new sentencing authority, we surveyed all 171 tribes that received federal funding that could have been used for indigent defense in any fiscal year from 2005 through 2010. In particular, we conducted a web-based survey to tribes that (1) reported allocating Tribal Priority Allocations (TPA)—federal funding that the Bureau of Indian Affairs (BIA) distributes to tribes and that tribes may allocate to a variety of activities—to their tribal courts (referred to as the "Tribal Courts TPA") (142 out of 171), (2) were awarded the Edward Byrne Memorial Justice Assistance Grant (JAG) by the Department of Justice (2 out of 171), or (3) both allocated funding to their Tribal Courts TPA and received JAG funding (27 out of 171) in any fiscal year from 2005 through 2010. We sent one survey to tribes that reported allocating TPA funding to Tribal Courts, and a separate survey to tribes that received JAG. For tribes that received both surveys, we asked that one representative from the tribe complete the section related to TLOA. We received responses from 109 tribes, for a response rate of 64 percent; however, not all 109 respondents answered every question. Our survey was composed of closed- and open-ended questions. In this enclosure, we include all the survey questions and aggregate results of responses to the closed-ended questions related to TLOA; we do not provide information on responses provided to the open-ended questions.[37]

Section V: Tribal Law and Order Act

The Tribal Law and Order Act of 2010 (TLOA) provides for new sentencing authority for Indian Tribes, but included several requirements—some related to indigent defense—that must be fulfilled before that authority may be exercised. (TLOA, Pub. L. No. 111-211, among other things, amended the Indian Civil Rights Act of 1968, Pub. L. No. 90-284.)

1. Does your Tribe currently, or have plans to, exercise the new sentencing authority provided by TLOA?

	Number of respondents
☐ Currently exercise	0
☐ Have plans to exercise	36
☐ No plans to exercise	31
☐ Don't know	34
☐ Total	101

2. Listed below are the TLOA requirements for exercising the new sentencing authority. Regardless of whether your Tribe plans to exercise the new sentencing authority, does your Tribe currently, or have plans to, implement any of the following?

TLOA requirements for exercising new sentencing authority	Does your Tribe currently, or have plans to, implement this requirement?	Number of Respondents
a. Provide the defendant the right to effective assistance of counsel at least equal to that guaranteed in the U.S. Constitution.	☐ Currently implement	41
	☐ Have plans to implement	18
	☐ No plans to implement	21
	☐ Don't know	20
	Total	100
b. Provide an indigent defendant the assistance of a defense attorney licensed to practice by any U.S. jurisdiction, at the expense of the Tribal government.	☐ Currently implement	39
	☐ Have plans to implement	18
	☐ No plans to implement	24
	☐ Don't know	19
	Total	100
c. Require that the judge presiding over the criminal proceeding have sufficient legal training to preside over criminal proceedings.	☐ Currently implement	73
	☐ Have plans to implement	11
	☐ No plans to implement	10
	☐ Don't know	8
	Total	102
d. Require that the judge presiding over the criminal proceeding be licensed to practice law in any U.S. jurisdiction.	☐ Currently implement	53
	☐ Have plans to implement	13
	☐ No plans to implement	20
	☐ Don't know	15
	Total	101

TLOA requirements for exercising new sentencing authority	Does your Tribe currently, or have plans to, implement this requirement?	Number of Respondents
e. Prior to charging the defendant, make publicly available the Tribe's criminal laws, rules of evidence, and rules of criminal procedure.	☐ Currently implement	66
	☐ Have plans to implement	17
	☐ No plans to implement	8
	☐ Don't know	10
	Total	101
f. Maintain a record of the criminal proceeding, including an audio or other recording.	☐ Currently implement	85
	☐ Have plans to implement	6
	☐ No plans to implement	5
	☐ Don't know	6
	Total	102

3. What challenges, if any, may affect your Tribe's ability to exercise the new sentencing authority under TLOA? For example, challenges may include funding, changing Tribal codes, increasing jail capacity, etc.

4. If you have any additional comments or would like to explain any of your answers on TLOA's sentencing authority, please provide them in the box below.

5. What assistance, if any, would your Tribe like to receive from the United States government to help your Tribe exercise the new sentencing authority provided by TLOA?

End Notes

[1] See Pub. L. No. 111-211, tit. II, § 202, 124 Stat. 2258, 2262-63 (2010) (recognizing, for example, that Indian tribes have faced significant increases in instances of domestic violence, burglary, assault, and child abuse as a direct result of increased methamphetamine use on Indian reservations).

[2] GAO, *Indian Country Criminal Justice: Departments of the Interior and Justice Should Strengthen Coordination to Support Tribal Courts*. GAO-11-252 (Washington, D.C.: Feb. 14, 2011). "Indian country" refers to all land within the limits of any Indian reservation under the jurisdiction of the U.S. government, all dependent Indian communities within U.S. borders, and all existing Indian allotments, including any rights-of-way running through an allotment. See 18 U.S.C. § 1151.

[3] GAO, *Indigent Defense: DOJ Could Increase Awareness of Eligible Funding and Better Determine the Extent to Which Funds Help Support This Purpose*. GAO-12-569 (Washington, D.C.: May 9, 2012). We used "indigent defense" to refer to any direct and indirect activities that help ensure indigent defendants are afforded counsel in criminal cases. These activities may include hiring public defenders, investigators, or other support staff; providing training for public defenders; making technological improvements in defenders' offices or systems; or providing loan repayments to help retain public defenders.

[4] BIA publishes a list of all Indian tribes that are recognized and eligible to receive funding and services from BIA by virtue of their status as Indian tribes (referred to as "federally-recognized tribes"). We sent one survey to tribes that reported allocating TPA funding to Tribal Courts, and a separate survey to tribes that received JAG. For tribes that received both surveys, we asked that one representative from the tribe complete the section related to TLOA. We did not include Courts of Indian Offenses (referred to as "CFR courts") in our survey of tribal courts because CFR courts constitute direct services administered by BIA officials. Based on discussions with BIA officials, we also did not include tribal courts in BIA's Alaska region.

[5] See GAO-12-569.

[6] In addition, the target population was tribes using BIA or DOJ funding, and not all tribes. For example, in some instances, tribes may operate tribal courts without receiving JAG funding or allocating funding to the Tribal Courts TPA.

[7] The total does not equal 109 because, although 109 tribes responded to our survey, 8 did not respond to this question.

[8] TCCLA provides funding and technical assistance to assist tribal jurisdictions in improving their justice systems. See e.g. 25 U.S.C. § 3663 (authorizing tribal criminal assistance grants).

[9] See GAO, *Internal Control: Standards for Internal Control in the Federal Government*, GAO/AIMD-00-21.3.1 (Washington, D.C.: November 1999).

[10] For example, the Major Crimes Act, as amended, provides the federal government with criminal jurisdiction over Indians charged with felony-level offenses enumerated in the statute. See 18 U.S.C. § 1153. Such felony-level offenses include murder; manslaughter; maiming; felony provisions of the Sexual Abuse Act of 1986, as amended, incest; assault with intent to commit murder; burglary; and robbery, among others.

[11] See, e.g., *Santa Clara Pueblo v. Martinez*, 436 U.S. 49, 55-56 (1978) (citing *United States v. Wheeler*, 435 U.S. 313 (1978)). See also 25 U.S.C. § 1301(2) (defining an Indian tribe's power of self-government).

[12] See *United States, v. Lara*, 541 U.S. 193, 200-01 (2004) (referencing the Indian Commerce Clause, U.S. CONST., art. I, § 8, cl. 3, and the Treaty Clause, U.S. CONST. art II, § 2, cl. 2, as authority for the federal regulation of Indian affairs). The General Crimes Act, the Major Crimes Act, and Public Law 280 are the three federal laws central to the exercise of criminal jurisdiction in Indian country. See 18 U.S.C. §§ 1152 (codifying the General

Crimes Act, as amended), 1153 (codifying the Major Crimes Act, as amended), and 1162 (codifying Public Law 280, as amended).

[13] The exercise of criminal jurisdiction by state governments in Indian country may be generally summarized as being limited to two instances—where both the alleged offender and victim are non-Indian, or where a federal treaty or statute confers, or authorizes a state to assume, criminal jurisdiction over Indians in Indian country.

[14] See *Santa Clara Pueblo,* 436 U.S. at 55-58 (explaining that tribes, as separate sovereigns preexisting the Constitution, "have historically been regarded as unconstrained by those constitutional provisions specifically as limitations on federal or state authority" and that through 25 U.S.C. § 1302 (enacted as amended through Indian Civil Rights Act), "Congress acted to impose certain restrictions upon tribal governments similar, but not identical, to those contained in the Bill of Rights and the Fourteenth Amendment").

[15] See Pub. L. No. 90-284, tit. II, 82 Stat. 73, 77 (1968) (codified as amended at 25 U.S.C. §§ 1301-41).

[16] See 25 U.S.C. § 1302(a)(1), (8).

[17] See 25 U.S.C. § 1302(a)(6).

[18] A term of imprisonment in excess of 1 year may be imposed upon a convicted defendant if the defendant had been previously convicted of the same or a comparable offense by any jurisdiction in the United States (e.g., federal or state) or if the defendant is being prosecuted for an offense comparable to an offense that, in any U.S. or state jurisdiction, may be punishable by more than 1 year of imprisonment. See 25 U.S.C. § 1302(b)(1)-(2). Further, the maximum term of imprisonment that may be imposed in a criminal proceeding (i.e., where a defendant is charged with multiple offenses,) is 9 years. See 25 U.S.C. § 1302(a)(7)(D).

[19] Specifically, such an attorney must be licensed to practice law by any jurisdiction in the United States that applies appropriate professional licensing standards and effectively ensures the competence and professional responsibility of its licensed attorneys. See 25 U.S.C. § 1302(c)(2).

[20] See Pub. L. No. 111-211, tit. II, § 235, 124 Stat. at 2282-86 (establishing the Commission and, among other things, mandating that it submit a report to the President and Congress no later than 2 years after enactment of TLOA (enacted July 29, 2010) detailing the findings and conclusions of the Commission and recommendations for legislative and administrative actions the Commission considers appropriate).

[21] Through the Indian Self-Determination and Education Assistance Act of 1975, Pub. L. No. 93-638, 88 Stat. 2203, as amended, the federal government established a policy of Indian self-determination whereby tribes, with the support and assistance of the federal government, would be afforded an "effective and meaningful" role in planning, conducting, and administering programs and services previously administered by federal entities. See 25 U.S.C. § 450a. Tribes generally obtain funding to assume these functions pursuant to self-determination contracts or self- governance compacts negotiated and entered into with BIA. See 25 U.S.C. §§ 450h, 458cc. Self-governance compacts differ from self-determination contracts in that such compacts afford tribes more flexibility in how the agreed upon funding may be utilized.

[22] See 25 U.S.C. § 2802.

[23] In fiscal year 2011, tribes could choose to allocate BIA funding to 34 TPA activities, including social services, natural resources management, and tribal courts.

[24] See 25 U.S.C. § 3665a.

[25] The total does not equal 109 because, although 109 tribes responded to our survey, 8 did not respond to this question.

[26] As we reported in February 2011, some tribes do not require that judges be law-trained or licensed to practice law. Rather, in many instances, qualifications to serve as a tribal judge may only include that the individual be a member of the tribe and meet any residency or age requirements established by the tribe.

[27] GAO-12-569.

[28] In addition, BIA provides direct services operations for those tribes that choose not to operate the program themselves, such as tribes that use CFR courts.

[29] In fiscal year 2010, DOJ awarded $25 million to tribes through the Tribal Court Assistance Program (TCAP), and $1.1 million through the Tribal Juvenile Accountability Discretionary Grant (TJADG). Starting in fiscal year 2010, TCAP and TJADG were rolled into CTAS, which includes one solicitation for 10 previously separate grant programs. The purpose areas related to justice systems include justice systems and alcohol and substance abuse, corrections and correctional alternatives, and violence against women. The purpose areas related to juvenile systems include juvenile justice and tribal youth courts.

[30] The AOUSC serves the federal judiciary in carrying out its constitutional mission to provide equal justice under law through a wide range of administrative, legal, financial, management, program, and information technology services to the federal courts. The U.S. Attorneys are the chief federal law enforcement officers in their districts, responsible for federal criminal prosecutions and civil cases involving the United States government.

[31] The other TCCLA categories are Category 1: Tribal Civil Legal Assistance Grants and Category 3: Tribal Justice Advocacy Training and Technical Assistance. Although Category 3 grants could be used to support tribes' efforts to exercise TLOA's sentencing authority, applicants are limited to national or regional membership organizations and associations whose membership section consists of judicial system personnel within tribal justice systems.

[32] The fiscal year 2010 solicitation stated that eligibility is "limited to tribal and non-tribal non-profit entities that provide legal assistance services for Indian tribes, members of Indian tribes, or tribal justice systems pursuant to federal poverty guidelines."

[33] See GAO/AIMD-00-21.3.1.

[34] Moreover, DOJ's Bureau of Justice Statistics is developing a national survey on tribal courts to be fielded in fiscal year 2013. DOJ officials stated that they intend to use the results from the survey to inform policy decisions, but because the survey is still being developed, they could not provide specific details regarding how the information will be used.

[35] Tribes, however, have the authority to move funds out of the Tribal Courts TPA into other TPA activities, such as social services.

[36] The National Judicial College offers programs to judges nationwide to improve the delivery of justice and advance the rule of law through a disciplined process of professional study and collegial dialogue. Since June 2002, it has included curricula aimed at the challenges facing tribal courts.

[37] Both surveys contained five sections: (1) awareness of allowable uses of funding; (2) allocation of funding for indigent defense; (3) conditions influencing whether funding was allocated for indigent defense; (4) likelihood of allocating 2011 funding for indigent defense; and (5) TLOA. For survey results and questions from the non-TLOA sections, see *Indigent Defense: Surveys of Grant Recipients, Select Tribes, and Indigent Defense Providers*, GAO-12-661SP (Washington, D.C.: May 2012). For a more detailed discussion of our survey methodology, see GAO-12- 569.

INDEX

C

D

H

I

J

K

L

Q

R

S

T

U

V

W

Y